—— THE ——
ULTIMATE GUIDE
TO
SELLING
YOUR HOME

How the Nation's Top Agents Break Records

Featuring **CRAIG SCHNEIDER**

REGS Publishing
Dallas, TX

ISBN: 978-1-64649-181-0

All proceeds from the sale of this book go to feed, clothe, and educate children in need around the globe.

Printed in the United States

CONTENTS

FOREWORD

As of June 2021, the National Association of Realtors has 1,504,474 members. That is to say a little over 1.2% of all working adults in America have a real estate license and are dues-paying members of the national professional association.

Let that sink in. More than one out of every 100 working adults claims, on some level, to be able to expertly advise, lead, guide, and protect you, the home buyer and home seller, as you make one of the largest family and financial decisions of your life.

The scary part is that it feels like even more people than that are shoving their business cards into your purse or pocket, asking for referrals, and reminding you to have your sister-in-law call when she's ready to sell her house. Picture in your mind right now how many people you know who are involved in residential real estate, as an agent, either part-time or full-time. You probably know a dozen or more.

It is therefore no great mystery why so many homeowners and soon-to-be homeowners think very little of real estate agents, and give serious thought to avoiding them altogether.

What you are holding in your hands is rare. This is a collection of wise and trustworthy instructions, woven together with stories and context by a hand-selected group of masterful real estate agents who defy the historically accurate stereotype that a large majority are not that great at their job. The chapters that follow are glimpses into the systems, marketing plans, and strategies of the most authoritative and credible experts in residential real estate in America.

You'll be able to take these proven strategies and implement them all by yourself. If you choose to buy or sell a home or investment property without a professional agent on your side, they will work in that manner. However, I will be direct and tell you right up front that I do not recommend it. I believe you'll get far better results if you find real estate agents like those generously contributing to this book with zero financial incentive to do so and have them put their full-time energy and full-time focus into creating abnormally positive results for you.

If you find yourself fortunate enough to live or have property or have interest in investing in a local real estate market where one of these gifted leaders lives and works, I'd strongly encourage you to reach out directly and to make use of their incredible track records and proven systems for success.

In my two decades in this business I've been on a crusade to move our industry professionals toward the high-quality standards, practices, and results of full-time CPAs, attorneys, and doctors. Knowing that those industries require significantly higher barriers to entry through rigorous education, apprenticeships, practicums, residencies, and more, real estate has a large gap to bridge.

I've written myself about the lies our industry tells new professionals, the unnecessary complexity shrouding the opportunities for everyday citizens to build wealth through real estate, and the fantastic benefits of home ownership and building a life of impact and purpose in and around the home. Through books, radio, events, media, and more, I've strained my voice to tell the American public that there are great professionals worthy of their respect and trust. However few and far between they are... they do exist. This book is proof.

Read it cover to cover so you know what is possible and even probable with great guidance. Read it and take notes on the wisdom and creativity that can propel you to a unique life in an ideal setting, building a wonderful future. Read it and see that real estate agents are not all the same, are not commodities but are world changers in more ways than one.

You'll see how some agents put tens of thousands of dollars of equity seemingly created out of thin air into their clients' pockets with brilliant marketing and negotiation strategies.

You'll see how others find properties that were otherwise unfindable by home buyers looking online, on the streets, and with other agents.

You'll learn how some agents even weave financing, development, and international business to create dream scenarios and legacy properties for clients who dream big or need big solutions to big property challenges.

Whatever you do, read this book, share it with those you like and love, and live a big, generous, purposeful life like these amazing authors do.

—TODD TRAMONTE
Author of *Live Free* and
5 Lies That Will Ruin Your Real Estate Career

SELLING THE "LIFESTYLE"
OF YOUR HOME

WITH CRAIG SCHNEIDER

CRAIG SCHNEIDER is the Founder and CEO of NORCHAR. He set out to create an industry-disrupting brokerage with a focus on providing world-class value. Since its inception in 2014, NORCHAR has done that and much more, ranking among the top 10 Real Estate Brokerage Firms within their market in New York.

After 10 years of honorable active military service, Craig resigned from his career as an Electronics Engineer to pursue his true passion in real estate. His experience is derived from being a top-producing sales agent for the market's largest developers and home builders.

Aside from being very personable, Craig is known for leveraging his strategic negotiation skills and impressive depth and breadth of market knowledge to his clients' benefit. This has earned him a sterling reputation for collaborating with his impressive network of buyers, sellers, and colleagues to seamlessly close over 1,800 straightforward to complex transactions.

Under Craig's leadership and standards of excellence NORCHAR has grown to be one of the largest and most innovative indie real estate firms in New York. NORCHAR's success has established Craig as a visionary and respected business leader in Rochester. Through his creative marketing savvy, Craig recognizes the importance of presenting every property to its best advantage. NORCHAR's fresh and unique approach to real estate marketing has transformed how homes are bought and sold in Upstate New York.

His philanthropic passion is to completely eliminate child hunger giving through NORCHAR's Social Mission, a partnership with Foodlink.

www.norchar.com
craig@norchar.com
(585) 333-2906

SELLING THE "LIFESTYLE" OF YOUR HOME

I believe you can change the outcome of any real estate transaction by focusing on the narrative. All homes have a story to tell, and you can create a clear vision of your home's lifestyle features.

It was a typical autumn weekend in New York, and with a brand new Real Estate license and a Saturday jam-packed with showings I had little foresight of the impact this day would have on my career. The market conditions favored the buyer, and we had a lot of options to choose from. My clients, Mary and Doug, were experienced homebuyers transferring for a new job opportunity, and we had been out looking at homes the previous day.

This morning almost felt like déjà vu—all of the houses started blending together in a sea of vanilla. Some were the same home built by the same builder, just on different lots. They were just so generic. They had beautiful gourmet kitchens with granite countertops, stainless-steel appliances, a beautiful master bath and giant walk-in closet. Most also had finished basements with all the fixings including bars and home theaters.

All of these homes were nice, and the majority met the buyers' needs, but something was missing that felt soulless; nothing made any of the houses memorable.

Then came home #5... just one more to see before lunch. Mary started intense negotiations with the twin boys—

Happy Meals in exchange for good behavior. As I walked up to their rental vehicle, they were already apologizing for how bad this tour could go. "And if things get out of control, we might have to cut it short and make a run for the closest golden arches."

I remember the chaos of the situation. While they unloaded the troops, I prepared myself for the showing and reviewed my printed materials for the home. I had plenty of time because the twins refused to get out of the car. They were crying and chanting, "Hap-py Meal," at the same time.

I acted like everything was normal and looked down at my sheet, where in giant all-caps in a bold font, the private remarks read: "MR. CLEAN LIVES HERE." The image of a bald man in a white shirt beating me up because the twins destroyed his home instantly popped into my mind.

After additional review, I realized this home was the same floorplan and builder as the one we had just left. I looked up and was happy to see this one was grey instead of tan. When we started up the drive I led off with, "How do you like the grey color?"

Both Doug and Mary said, "I prefer tan – jinx!" Then Mary immediately followed by saying, "Isn't this the same house we just walked through?" As they started heading back to the rental car, I screamed, "Wait!" I didn't want to have to explain to a top-producing seller's agent why I set up a showing but my clients didn't take the tour. So I desperately needed to convince Doug and Mary to see the home anyway.

I opened my negotiations with the guilt that the sellers had spent time cleaning the home for the showing and concluded with offering to buy the kids' Happy Meals *plus* ice cream for the entire family.

While unlocking the front door and explaining it would only take five minutes, I shared that "Mr. Clean" lived in the home and that we needed to be on our best behavior. All the while I was thinking to myself, *"This is going to be impossible."* Nonetheless I shared a confident smile with Mary and Doug.

Upon entry, we were greeted by a smell I could only compare to fresh-baked pie. The seller had left all of the lights on for us, as well as nice background music coming from their TV. On the right was a formal dining room with the table set for dinner.

Around the corner to the left was a study that was being used as a playroom. The TV was on with cartoons playing and the seller's children had left a note on their chalkboard that read, "Please play with our toys." The twins couldn't read, however they jumped right in, just being kids. I saw this as an opportunity and offered to keep an eye on the boys while Doug and Mary enjoyed the home.

While trying to keep the twins distracted from seeing the giant Lego castle that I was afraid they would destroy, I remember hearing Mary say, "I absolutely love that," and "This is perfect." I figured they must like the selections in the kitchen.

After about thirty minutes I couldn't believe Mary and Doug were still looking at this home. I figured they just wanted a break from the twins and were taking advantage of my free babysitting service. Then one of the children started to get anxious.

At this point Doug and Mary returned to the makeshift playroom in a very positive mood. I blurted out, "Who's ready for a Happy Meal," in an effort to get the twins to stop screaming.

Mary said, "Before we go, I want to show you boys something." I think I was more surprised than the twins. I couldn't believe Mary was trying to hold us hostage to this home for one more minute.

She told us to grab our shoes, which we had taken off, and then we followed her through the kitchen to the rear patio door. I remember being confused because the kitchen was an exact replica of the home we had just seen. Mary guided us to the backyard where there was a portable gas firepit surrounded by Adirondack chairs and a few oversized boulders that looked like the homebuilder didn't want to move.

The seller had left the firepit on. On a small table they had laid out supplies to make s'mores with some disposable wooden sticks to roast marshmallows over the fire. The seller also left out some local craft pumpkin beers and cider from a local farmer's market. We only knew how close the farmer's market was because the seller had left a map showing its location.

At this point Mary shared with me a handwritten letter from the seller, which was what she had been referring to when she said, "I absolutely love that." The letter shared many stories of how great the home had been for their family, including stories of large parties held for their kids, and listing all the things they were going to miss when they left.

The seller went on to share why they originally picked the home and homesite, including a story about how they insisted the builder leave the big boulders in the backyard. On the map the sellers shared all of their favorite "secret" places including restaurants, grocers, and entertainment.

On the back of the handwritten note was a hand-drawn map of the neighborhood showing a path to a small, stocked pond. It looked like a pirate's treasure map to the twins. The last sentence of the note offered the use of their electric golf cart in the garage to go and explore the path and pond. I encouraged this exploration and said I would wait at the home for their return.

Twenty minutes passed. We had now long exceeded our allotted showing window. I was waiting for Mr. Clean to come home and ask me where his golf cart had disappeared to.

Then I realized the "Mr. Clean lives here" note is what had made me think the home was clean. However, on reflection it was similar in cleanliness to all the other houses we had looked at. This one just felt cleaner because they set that expectation.

Upon the family's return, the twins couldn't wait to share stories about their trip in the golf cart. Doug told me they wanted to write an offer. I asked if they still wanted to look at the three other homes on our list that were set up for that afternoon.

Mary looked at me. "We've already found our new home."

I was excited to do a deal with this top-producing listing agent, so I called to share that my buyers had an interest in the property. I wanted to see what terms would be important to the seller.

That was when the listing agent shared with me that he already had an offer in hand and was expecting another that day. I thought to myself, *"Wait a minute... how is this happening? It's a buyer's market and we are supposed to be calling the shots."* At the completion of my call, the listing agent said they would be reviewing offers at 6:00 P.M. and to be sure I had my offer in by then.

I called Doug to explain what was happening. He asked me what they needed to do to get the home. I shared with him that I needed to consult someone I trusted, and that I would be in touch soon, so we agreed to meet in my office an hour later.

I called my attorney and explained the situation, asking what would be our best course of action. He suggested writing an offer that included an escalation clause that would raise the price above and beyond any competing offers up to a maximum price of my buyers' choice.

In that moment, I thought I had a spark of brilliance—home #4 had been the exact same house... actually better because the buyers both preferred tan siding. So I called the listing agent and asked if they had any offers on that one. She explained that they didn't and encouraged me to submit one. I couldn't wait to share my genius with Doug and Mary.

I couldn't have been more prepared for their return. I even had coloring books at the ready for the twins. Once seated I started to share with them how I came up with an amazing idea. I explained that house #4 was exactly the same as house #5 and actually better because it was tan. That home was within half a mile of the other one. I remember feeling so smart, because I was going to save them thousands of dollars.

I'll never forget the look Mary gave me. Even the twins glanced up from their coloring books to shake their heads in disgust. Doug thanked me for trying to come up with options, however they wanted home #5 and asked what needed to be done to get it.

I shared that we could do this new thing called an "escalation clause" and we called my attorney to explain all the details. He wound up busy that weekend, not only explaining what an escalation clause was to me and my clients, but also to the listing agent and his broker. In the end we won the home and Mary and Doug couldn't have been happier.

After closing I asked why the preference for home #5. Mary shared that it just felt like home.

That was when I realized the power of selling the lifestyle of the home. Both houses were identical. I even later discovered that home #4 had access to a similar stocked pond. I also realized that many of the features the buyers fell in love with on home #5 were not included with the sale—like the portable firepit and electric golf cart. They also weren't buying things like the proximity of the fishpond or farmer's market.

Doug later told me the sellers had left out an old fishing pole with a lure on the golf cart, so when they had made their way up to the fishpond that first afternoon, Doug and the boys gave that pole a quick cast. The twins were so excited to catch their first fish. Still to this day, I share that this was the lure that made the sale.

Being responsible for over 1,800 sales since that jam-packed Saturday, I'm still fixated on helping my sellers focus on their home's "lifestyle" story. My obsession became the catalyst of what turned into an incubator of like-minded top-producing real estate professionals that identified six pre-listing steps that are essential to selling the lifestyle of your home.

6 essential pre-listing steps to selling the "lifestyle" story of your home for maximum price in minimal time

Step 1
Inspect—Clean—Declutter

The difference between a 4-star and a 5-star restaurant is the attention to detail. I believe this same principal carries over to listing and marketing your home. It starts with a pre-inspection of the property by a qualified professional home inspector. Doing so shifts control to you the seller, enabling you to save money by making small repairs up front while at the same time giving you control of information and the ability to eliminate deal killers.

You will also want to professionally deep clean your home before you start building your media collection for marketing. It is essential that your home is at its absolute cleanest when it hits the market. It is strongly recommended that you bring in a team of professionals who have been trained and have the proper tools to make your home sparkle and smell nice. This team will make sure all of the windows are clean inside and out, and that ceiling fan blades, baseboards, horizontal surfaces, window blinds, light bulbs/fixtures, and all vents including HVAC and bath fans are dust-free. The cleaners will also pay special attention in the kitchen and bathrooms to make sure everything that is supposed to shine shines.

Most buyers are unable to judge the construction quality of a home due to inexperience in that profession, however almost all buyers know the difference between a clean home and a dirty home. The reason this is important to understand is that buyers associate the quality of your home's build and maintenance with its cleanliness, so if your home is dirty, they will assume you have also not maintained the property. Clean homes sell quicker and for more money.

To declutter your space, start in the closets. You can prepack off-season outfits and donate clothing you have not worn since high school. Almost any "collection" of anything should be prepacked and stored away—beanie babies are unfortunately a distraction when trying to highlight the features of your home. Pack them up so you can enjoy them at your next home. A professional stager will be able to assist with suggestions on what to keep and what to store.

Step 2
Stage—Repair—Improve

Real Estate agents say it all the time... "Buyers tend to be more emotional, and sellers tend to be more analytical." When you're selling your home's "lifestyle" story, you tap into the psychology that a buyer will fall in love with. It's a narrative that lets buyers envision themselves living in your home. Even for new houses, builders will sell you on the walking trails and the distance from the best restaurants.

With over 18 years of experience in new construction sales and past exposure to national homebuilders' sales centers, I spent tremendous amounts of focus and energy on creating the lifestyle story around the community and not just the home level. Every detail is important.

When writing up directions to your home, choose the nicest route—not always the shortest. Disney World does this by guiding you through the main gates or grand hotel entrance. I am sure you would agree your Disney experience would be much different if you entered through the rear gates next to the trash dumpsters.

Help your buyers see the lifestyle by creating marketing that provides a tour of your community. Pay special attention to social opportunities or things that are tied to a buyer's lifestyle goals. Point out that your neighborhood has sidewalks and streetlights that encourage neighbors to get out and meet. Help the buyer see themselves strolling around your neighborhood talking to all of the neighbors.

If there is an amazing outdoor restaurant that you absolutely love, make this part of the buyer's experience by pointing it out. The juicier the story, the better. Provide a gift card so they can experience it for themselves.

If your property has a lemon tree, you might leave out some fresh-squeezed lemonade and explain that most of the year you make yours from the fruit of this tree. Your goal is to make it very easy for the buyer to see themselves living the lifestyle within your home.

You don't even have to own the stuff you're selling. For example, you don't own the town parks, nice restaurants, or the neighbor who gives out full-size candy bars at Halloween. However these are the items that make your neighborhood unique. If you package that into the buyer's emotional buy-in, then they'll pay more, pay faster, and with less drama.

A professional stager is different than a decorator. Decorators have been trained to help you decorate your home in a unique style that is unique to your tastes. Stagers have been formally trained to make a home marketable to an audience of prospective homebuyers. Stagers can help point out distractions in your home that can cost you thousands of dollars in the final sales price. They can also help a buyer see themselves living in your home by creating stories throughout, making sure each room has a clear identity by adding items that provide value and removing those that distract from the story.

Stagers help the audience of potential buyers see the value of living in your home and envision themselves in your home on a daily basis enjoying those highlighted features with friends and family.

The stager and professional home inspector will provide you with suggested improvements and repairs that can add thousands to the value of your home. You should identify a plan to complete these improvements and repairs prior to building your media marketing materials. If you expect a buyer to pay top dollar for your home, you need to give them a top-dollar experience. Completing these items prior to listing will reduce drama during the sales process and give you the upper hand in negotiation.

Step 3
Seller Interview — Write the Story — Build a Lifestyle
The best story wins, so you need to identify who the buyer is and what is going to be important to them. When you're thinking about selling your house, you've got to get inside your ideal buyer's mind and figure out how to make them fall in love with your home.

Buyers don't necessarily need a guru. They just need to be emotionally attached. They need someone who can help guide them through a journey. Make it easy for them to experience your home's authentic lifestyle story by first identifying a list of twenty items you would like to imprint on all buyers. You, the seller, should be involved in the process of developing this list because nobody has a better understanding of your home and area than you... the actual person who has lived there for 10 or 20 or 30 years.

Create a list of questions and have a friend come over to interview you and the other family members who live in the home. One question I always enjoy asking my clients is: "What are five adjectives that describe your home?" Other great questions include: "Why did you buy this home?" "What is something that surprised you about living here and has been impactful to your life?" and "What will you miss most about this home, neighborhood, community?"

This interview is designed to help identify those lifestyle items that you can build a story around—like that little deli around the corner or the secret place you go to collect lost golf balls on the course behind your home, enabling you to never have the need to purchase golf balls. These are the things that are going to emotionally connect the buyer and give them the desire to want to live in your home.

As the seller you should consider writing the buyer a letter about what you love about your home. Share your home's "greatest hits"—things you have done at your home that a buyer might be able to easily replicate. Including some photos of these events can be helpful in creating a vision.

Once you have your story figured out, try to mix in things that are relevant in the news or that people are talking about on a daily basis to create buzz. Some of my past customers have used things like: *Wait until you see this "Kardashian closet" or "Gaines-inspired shiplap wall."* If you're marketing to the correct audience, they will not only appreciate these lifestyle features, they will seek them out.

Step 4
Multi-Media Package

You need amazing content to build a story around lifestyle. It should start with professional architectural photography. These photos will be the first showing of your property that buyers see on the internet. What is important is having great photos with the highest quality, equal to photos you'd see in a magazine.

Today's content-consuming buyers expect more digital content like 360-tours and drone photography and video. Your goal is to provide enough teaser content to keep them coming back to consume this information multiple times, because the more often they see it, the more they will emotionally connect to the home.

Having high-quality photos, video, and drone images will enable you to build out additional amazing content, including social media and print materials. The photos you put on the internet should be just a teaser. Your first six photos should tell the story. They don't need to be in order, but they should be your absolute best photos that leave the buyer begging for more.

Step 5
Refine—Scarcity—Urgency

Unlike traditional real estate agents, your goal is to sell the lifestyle story of your home so you can find not just any buyer for your home, but rather the ideal buyer. The reason is critical. Your ideal buyer will pay more, pay faster, and create less drama. You accomplish this by identifying those buyers and then building a marketing plan to reach them.

Tailoring our storytelling and marketing to that ideal buyer and getting it in front of their eyeballs—through venues where these buyers already hang out—helps you find someone who is already prone to buying and likely to fall in love with the lifestyle story you're about to tell.

If you're selling the outdoor experiences lifestyle because of the location of your home, look for people who are already enthusiastic about outdoor experiences. Find them and then weave in where they shop, what they read, what they watch, and what excites them, and meet them there.

Generating scarcity means creating a market of one. Doing this at a high level creates unbelievable results. Focus on the unique niches for your home. The more unusual, the better. I believe that your home's oddities become its commodities. Build stories around the unique features of your home and then explain the benefit of those features to your buyer, allowing them to see themselves in that lifestyle.

Scarcity comes in the form of you selling a lifestyle while your neighbors are just selling a house.

You can communicate scarcity by showing customers what others are doing in real-time. You can accomplish this by controlling showing windows and stacking viewings of your property. When buyers are able to see what other buyers are doing, it gives them an idea that they need to act quickly.

Experience has shown that customers have a more positive reaction when they are shown what they will lose if they don't buy a home, rather than what they will gain if they do. If you are selling a home in an area that has special financing available or grant money available, ask the potential buyers how much they would lose by continuing to rent, building equity for their landlord instead of themselves.

Some say scarcity involves pressure and even stress or fear, to push people to make a purchase. In truth, scarcity is a reward for those who act fast. If your home's lifestyle story is compelling, the marketing is done well, and your home is top notch, then the real result is simply a reward for your home's biggest fan—a buyer who unconditionally loves your home's story and doesn't need time to think about it.

Too much pressure is a bad thing, though. Be sure to use scarcity-focused strategies in moderation. They should always be genuine in nature. When you put too much pressure on buyers to act, they feel like you're forcing them into action and not letting them make their own decisions... resulting in no offer being submitted. It is best to develop a balanced plan of scarcity and urgency throughout your marketing plan. Providing smaller, digestible opportunities for the buyer to say yes will reward you with an offer.

Step 6
Pricing
When it comes to establishing a price for your home, there is not a single one-size-fits-all approach. Homes are unique, one-of-a-kind items each having characteristics that add or subtract from their value. You must also consider that the market is elastic, and these values are always adjusting. Some markets and neighborhoods are more predictable than others.

Know your audience. The buyer market is identified by those who are ready, willing, and able. Your home is worth as much as the market is willing to pay for it, not its replication cost, not what you owe on the mortgage, or what you initially paid. You serve your home's market, and you need to establish a price that is within the tolerance of that active market.

Unfortunately, many homeowners don't believe this. They think their pride-and-joy family home of 30 years is worth more. Others want to "test the limits" of the market to squeeze a few extra dollars out of their biggest financial asset. But to market your house competitively, you need to set a price based on the facts. Think seasonality, local market conditions, and your home's unique characteristics above the value of memories and emotions.

Because property values are hyperlocal and always shifting, you should consider comparable sales, aka "comps," when establishing a price range for your home. This allows you to compare your home side-by-side against other recently sold properties similar to yours in location, size, and condition. This also enables you to size up the competition and nail down a price range, from which you can add or subtract value based on your home's unique positioning, features, upgrades, and lifestyle story.

House comps also put a reality check on your rosy-eyed views of the home that holds so many memories. When trying to get top dollar, you need to consider how your home's condition compares with the competition. Often sellers fail to take into account that the neighbor just invested $150,000 into remodeling work on the home they sold, and unless you are willing to do the same, you can't expect the same results.

That doesn't mean you should spend months remodeling every room in your home just to raise the asking price. That would require going head-to-head with professionals like investors and home flippers who have more money, time, and experience in the business of turning a profit on home renovations. You're better off using the comps to set a price range and keeping major projects to a minimum.

To command your full asking price, be sure to create a compelling lifestyle story. Get the house show-ready by completing the list of minor changes you received from your home inspector and stager, and don't forget to deep clean every room and declutter.

Where can I get help?

These six-steps to selling the lifestyle story of your home are the foundation of a much larger system we developed for our clients. I would love to say that creating a lifestyle story and then marketing it to capture the right eyes is simple, but we have a group of really talented professionals who help make it feel easy. There is a lot of moving parts and we try to remove the pain from the process by being very systemized and making sure all of our listings receive the same high level of service.

Over the years, we have needed to create a team of highly trained professionals to deliver this unique level of service. For us to do this consistently with predictable results, we have brought most of the services in-house. This is the only way we could achieve quality results while keeping costs affordable. We provide all of these services for our clients, because experience shows the client generally won't do it for themselves or they try to skimp.

Don't shortchange yourself or the buyer of your home by not taking the time to create an experience worth sharing while celebrating your home's lifestyle story!

HOW TO SELL YOUR VACATION HOME FROM YOUR MAIN HOME

WITH BRIAN WITT

BRIAN WITT was born and raised in beautiful Bozeman, MT. His family roots extend six generations through Montana soil. With that type of family legacy, he is deeply committed to preserving what makes Montana special while also looking to the future.

As a third-generation Realtor his family has dedicated their lives to serving others. They have persisted through 12 recessions, watched the state's economy change from a heavy mining/industry and agricultural production, to becoming a prime relocation state and leader in tourism. They not only understand Montana history deeply but, more importantly, know its future better than anyone else.

Their clients have been with them through first home purchases, second home purchases, the purchasing of their first investment properties, development projects, and the passing of real estate assets to second and third generations. They are truly dedicated to serving you for life.

www.bison-realty.com
brian@bison-realty.com
(406) 285-8546

HOW TO SELL YOUR VACATION HOME FROM YOUR MAIN HOME

Thanks to the power of the internet, it can be a very simple process to sell your vacation property even when you do not live nearby. You and your Realtor can hop on a phone call or a Zoom chat to discuss all the options of listing your property. Contracts can be signed no matter where you are in the world, including out of the country. The only issue then is the time difference!

When you have a local expert's help, it is simple to sign a contract and get your property listed. What we provide is really a concierge level of service, so you as the seller never have to be onsite.

We handle the cleaning, staging, marketing, and get the photos taken care of for you. We also set up closing at a title company nearby to where you currently reside... or we can even send out a mobile notary to work with you in the comfort of your own home. We handle all of that!

Before going to market

If major repairs need to be done on a property, it's always best to have those taken care of before the listing goes live. It generally takes a couple of weeks to list a property using the higher level of marketing you're reading about in this book, so all repairs can be done concurrently with that.

Otherwise, all the aspects of preparation for listing your property are included in our services.

Pre-inspection?

We recommend that you do hire a home inspector ahead of time, just so there are no surprises. Once we get into a contract with a buyer, things like foundation issues, roofing issues, or mold should never pop up. Those are major deal killers. Most buyers are simply not willing to overlook them.

However, if you as the seller take the opportunity to know about those things in advance, you can mitigate them before they ever become a problem. Get a clean bill of health from a roofing contractor, a mold remediation specialist, or a structural engineer to say that everything is in tip-top shape. Then a buyer won't have reservations or feel you're intentionally trying to mislead them.

Once a buyer discovers a major issue that hasn't been disclosed up front, they will start to look for other issues that might be hidden. But the reverse is also true... when we disclose all of that up front, their confidence goes up and so does the property value.

What's included?

These are seven primary things we're going to do for you that you won't need to:

1. We manage a pre-inspection, which could lead to your ability to make repairs before listing, as mentioned above.

2. We manage the staging of the property, whether vacant or furnished.

3. We manage the photography, which could include video and drone photography.

4. We market the property in multiple ways.

5. We strategically place the home on the market on certain days to ensure your home hits the market with the highest possible demand.

6. We coordinate all property viewings and keep open lines of communication with other agents from the first showing, through the offering process, during the contract contingency periods, and fully through closing. We are excellent communicators and are fully transparent!

7. Our extensive relationships with experts of all types related to home sales help ensure solutions to problems as they arise and a seamless transaction from start to finish.

What to disclose to a buyer

With a second home or vacation property, it's important to disclose that the home is not your primary residence, or that you may not have visited the property in quite a while. The owner's Property Disclosure in the state of Montana already has a line for this type of disclosure. It makes the process very simple.

There are certain things above a cosmetic level of defect that a buyer must be made aware of. But if, as we recommend, you hire a home inspector beforehand, you will have already mitigated those items before the property is even listed.

How to maximize the sale price

There are several things you can do to maximize the sale price of a home before it goes to market, including having the interior professionally cleaned and removing all personal photographs.

We help stage your home to make it appear like a Ritz-Carlton level hotel. Anyone who walks into it can envision themselves living in the property. If you have quirky wall colors, those should be replaced with a more neutral tone. If there are major blemishes on a refrigerator, it may be worthwhile to have that item replaced. If hardwood floors show heavy wear, it would be a good idea to have those refinished while we're working out the listing. However, if you're working with a concierge-level service like mine, you're not going to have to do much because we'll take care of all that for you.

Second, it's good to see if it's worth adding any positives to the property before listing. If the home has dated countertops, it may be cost-effective to update those depending on market conditions. A great local agent who knows that market can help you make these decisions.

What to leave behind

Typically items that are bolted to a wall are considered part of the home. So if there's a family heirloom, for example, that you wish to keep, it's important to disclose that the item will not be staying in the property.

Essentially you can take whatever you want as long as you properly disclose it up front. A great agent can craft the negotiation in a way that protects you and your assets. This is more relevant in second home deals, as in this type of transaction buyers often make a purchase for a fully furnished property.

If an item is not attached to the wall, your buyer may expect it to not be included in the sales price. As a funny (not-funny) example, we've had multimillion-dollar deals fall apart because of a $400 clothes dryer, or come together because the seller was willing to leave a $900 projector. It's crazy.

We can do whatever is needed, as long as we know and disclose it up front. Many times, for the right price, the seller chooses to just leave all their stuff. This helps a buyer for whom the property will not become a primary residence, because then they don't have to buy all that extra furniture and decorations. So you as the seller can keep that one painting and great-grandma's afghan, but include all the rest of your stuff—without needing to pack anything up!

The right agent will be able to assist and handle all of this for you.

The system in action

I recently had a sale which involved both an out-of-state buyer and an out-of-state seller. Because of our highly effective marketing, we ended up with 13 offers—above asking price—which led to a 14% increase in the sales price of the home. Wow! And this client accomplished it without stepping foot on the property.

The seller lived more than a thousand miles away. The property they wanted to sell was a multimillion-dollar home. Due to their massive success in their profession, and the lockdown during the pandemic, their ability to travel to Montana was not possible. The heaviest lifting that was

required of them was mailing a key to put in a lock box...
We handled everything else for them.

HOW TO WIN
WHEN SELLING
IN A TIME OF DISTRESS

WITH *THERESA BASTIAN*

THERESA BASTIAN is a seasoned Realtor with over 20 years of success working with buyers, sellers, and investors. Past clients rave about her ability to serve their needs, whether they're buying or selling. She helps her clients make educated choices about one of the most important financial and personal decisions of their lives. Her ability to help divorcing couples untangle their real estate holdings has been recognized by *Texas Realtor Magazine* and she has provided expert witness testimony on property valuation for divorce hearings and mediations.

Theresa enjoys spending time serving her community in many ways. She is currently the Secretary/Treasurer of the Board of Directors for the Travis County Appraisal District.

She also serves on the Grievance Committee for the State Bar of Texas and chairs the Legislative Management Committee for the Austin Board of REALTORS®.

But above all of these accomplishments, her proudest role is mom. Theresa's son Lukas is a United States Marine and her daughter Sophia currently attends the University of Arkansas.

www.letsmoveaustin.com
theresa@letsmoveaustin.com
(512) 297-3442

HOW TO WIN
WHEN SELLING
IN A TIME OF DISTRESS

The most common types of hardship when selling a home that I have run across in my more than 20-year real estate practice are people experiencing financial hardship or emotional stress due to death, illness, or job loss, or people going through divorce, which is often a combination of both financial and emotional stress. All of these life situations force people to reevaluate where they are with their financial situation and housing. Most often these situations are not intended—which means they were not planned for.

I have been divorced twice myself. The second time was especially devastating since I was forced to walk away from a business and home we owned together. I wasn't sure I would ever recover from that financially (or emotionally, for that matter). But I have, thankfully, and I've made it my mission to help others going through difficult situations like divorce and financial hardship so they can see there is light on the other side of that tunnel.

The biggest mistakes

Selling a home during a time of financial or emotional distress or divorce is entirely different than a "regular" sale. Typically, when a family or individual decides to sell their home, it's because they're moving toward something more exciting. Perhaps it's an opportunity to move for a job transfer or better school district, or maybe it's to finally get that house with a pool or the acreage you've always wanted. These types of moves are something sellers have planned for, maybe even dreamed about. It's also a plan that likely occurred over a longer period of time, sometimes years. But when people are forced to sell due to hardship, it is almost always a sudden, unexpected, and undesirable change.

Unfortunately, this short timeframe and lack of ability to prepare can cause sellers to make some pretty devastating mistakes. People who have to sell their homes in adverse hardship situations are typically highly stressed and emotional. They find themselves responding to decisions with knee-jerk reactions, limited creativity, and almost a sense of desperation. They are at risk of being taken advantage of because they feel overwhelmed, like they have no options. A dramatic change has been forced on them. They are eager to jump on the first solution that looks like a life preserver. For all these reasons they often become prey to an unethical segment of the real estate industry.

A distressed seller may think, *"Well, I can't afford to replace the carpets that the pets have ruined, and I can't install new appliances, so I'm not going to get very good money for my house."* Then when the first person comes around who offers them any price at all, they just agree to it. Sadly, there's a whole sector of this industry that thrives on people saying yes because they think they don't have any options. There are companies and people who deliberately use misleading marketing to prey on those in distress when they are likely to have high emotions and make impulsive decisions.

That just drives me insane, because you need to realize that even in a distressed situation you still have options! A good Realtor is going to relieve some of the decision-making burden. A professional Realtor will lay out the options so you can see what is legitimately possible so you don't end up settling for thousands and thousands less than you should. Without such expert help, the situation might snowball into your equity in the home being lost to foreclosure, or allowing your home fall into disrepair and lose value.

I honestly feel it's my calling to protect my clients from those who are out for a quick buck and have no problem taking advantage of people when they are most vulnerable. My goal is to take a bad situation and find a way for you to move forward from it into a brighter future, not to let a bad situation spiral into something even worse.

How to avoid getting taken advantage of

To avoid getting taken advantage of in times of vulnerability, a seller really needs a uniquely focused expert. You need to find someone who is passionate about helping you navigate the complexities of selling during a time of challenge—whether that means emotional or financial hardship, or a divorce. You should not just talk to one Realtor and agree to their first proposal. I understand that it's difficult to have the mental bandwidth to interview multiple agents, especially when you're already dealing with all of the things that go along with a divorce or declaring bankruptcy or a job loss. It can feel overwhelming to make those calls and set up appointments. If you really don't have the ability to do multiple interviews, I suggest you look for someone with expert training in working with distressed or divorcing homeowners.

Divorce concerns to keep in mind

I have earned the Certified Divorce Real Estate Expert designation. This means I am one of less than a hundred Realtors in the entire country who have gone through the training to successful facilitate the real estate aspects of a family law case. I also became a Certified Distressed Property Expert and have prevented hundreds of families from losing their homes to foreclosure during the financial downturn in 2008-2009. There are only a small number of agents who take the time and spend the money to get this specialized knowledge of how to navigate such serious situations.

You may be tempted to work with a neighbor down the street who dabbles in real estate on the side, or your mom's friend from church who has her real estate license but is mostly retired these days. There are a lot of wonderful, well-intentioned people out there who can be just as dangerous for you as the vultures.

These Realtors may well care about you, but do they have the experience and specific training to navigate the world of banks, short sales and pre-foreclosures?

Do they have the skillset to work with the world of family law and judicial orders?

They don't realize the complexity of family law issues, such as how to interpret a judicial order or negotiate when two spouses don't agree on what should happen next. And that inexperience can set off a cascade of events that results in a more difficult, time-consuming, stressful sale that ends up causing your house to sell for less money.

No money, time, or energy to fix up the home

Since every market and every situation is different, there is no one-size-fits-all answer to whether you need to invest the time and energy—and especially the money—to fix up a home before listing it for sale.

I can tell you that most properties that I'm brought in to assist with in a distressed selling situation do need work. I have created a system that outlines the top 3 scenarios that sellers in times of hardship should consider.

1. Sell as-is
2. Do a bare minimum of repairs
3. Execute a more extensive make-ready process

A good Realtor, a true professional, is going to be able to project what price you can expect to sell for and the timeline for each of these scenarios. I take all aspects of your unique situation into consideration, as well as all of the possible repairs and updates, then evaluate them on these factors:

1. The time involved
2. The energy involved
3. Will it make a difference to your bottom line, and if so, how much?

This way you can make an educated decision on how to proceed. I often negotiate with one of my preferred vendors to either get a discounted rate for distressed sellers or to postpone all or part of their fees to be paid at closing.

Basically, when you feel like you don't have any choices, I provide options. Life happens to everybody. It doesn't matter whether your job was downsized or your marriage ended—you don't deserve to lose your financial stability. And when you're embarrassed and overwhelmed and just trying to get through the day, I take the worry about selling the property and the next steps for your living situation off your plate.

A caregiver's crisis

I was able to help a woman whose parents lived out of state and were having major health problems. The client needed to move closer to her parents and felt completely guilty that she hadn't done this sooner. To make it worse, she'd lost her job the previous year and had gone through almost all of her savings.

Her house was in poor condition, but she didn't have the time, funds, or mental energy to prepare it for a sale. When I met her she was seriously considering walking away and letting the bank foreclose. This would have been such a mistake! She had built up almost $200k of equity in the house! Even selling as-is would have been better than walking away! But I knew that it would be a highly marketable property if we could just get the basics done for the next buyer.

I earned her trust and put a plan together that allowed her to pack up her personal items and valuables that she wanted to take with her so she could get on the road to be with her parents.

With her permission, I acted as the project manager and arranged for new carpet and paint, a landscaping refresh, and to have the remaining household items donated.

Even after she paid these expenses from the proceeds of the sale, she profited over $150k—money she really needed.

And now she doesn't have a foreclosure on her record! I felt honored to have had the chance to help her get a fresh start.

SELLING IN A COLLEGE TOWN

WITH JOHN BYERS

JOHN BYERS has been in real estate since 2002. After graduating from Texas A&M University, he took a Commission with the United States Air Force, attaining the rank of Captain. He later moved to Houston, TX, where he began working for State Farm Insurance. State Farm relocated him to the College Station/Bryan area and into a technology training position.

After ten years in the corporate world, John decided to pursue a career in real estate. He has co-owned three national real estate franchises and now owns one of the fastest growing independent brokerages in College Station, TX.

He is married to Cindy, and they have two beautiful daughters, Elizabeth and Rebekah. John enjoys leading in his church's Singles Ministry and traveling with his family.

Their goal is to visit all 50 states before the girls graduate college. When not working in real estate or traveling, you will find John at home working on his farm just outside College Station.

www.towerpointteam.com
john@towerpointteam.com
(979) 412-1601

SELLING IN A COLLEGE TOWN

College towns are unique and can be confusing at times. It is my desire to help you understand the opportunities a college town possesses and walk away with a worthwhile selling strategy.

Before we head into real estate, we need to understand that the college town is a uniquely American invention. Universities were created in Europe. The schools were typically in large cities because that is where the educators were. The students came to them.

Harvard, the very first U.S. college (now a university), was located five miles outside of Boston. The intention was to distance the students from the distractions city life provided. That is why America has so many schools in smaller towns.

The U.S. is a vast country and needed colleges across the nation available to the people. The difference then between a college town versus a college in a large metropolitan city like Houston, Dallas, or Boston today is the college continues to dramatically affect the makeup and character of the community.

Texas A&M University (TAMU) in College Station, TX, where I am located, was built 5-7 miles from the nearest town. Bryan, TX, was not far, but it was far enough away that the area around the train station where students got dropped off that it took on a life of its own and became a town. The college train station became known as College

Station, demonstrating just how integrated a school and town can be.

Today College Station, TX, is a market area of about 150,000 in population and has everything from private companies investing in virology and pharmaceutical research and manufacturing, ocean exploration and geosciences partnerships for ocean drilling expeditions, to nanofabrication laboratories. There is even a nuclear reactor on campus as well as one of the largest atomic particle colliders in the world. A recent investment has been in the health science center in our small town which now draws even more scientists and healthcare workers to the area. All this demonstrates how the college can influence the character of a town.

Local activities are affected as well. How many small towns offer Off-Broadway performing arts, four world-class golf courses, a presidential library, five art galleries, and SEC athletic events? We have football, basketball, baseball, tennis, track... even a polo team as well as a regional airport on campus to get you in and out.

The types of businesses and partnerships that a college town can support are totally different from those that would come to a "normal" small town of similar size.

Typically, the feel of the area is more youthful, and significantly more educated. The over-65 population is easily four to five percentage points higher in larger cities than in a college town. While smaller towns do not typically attract a youthful crowd, they flock to a university town. The median age of College Station, TX, or another college town like Stillwater, OK, is 23... while Dallas, TX, or Boston, MA, is more than ten years older.

An additional difference is the education level of the people in a college town. According to Census.gov those over 25 in College Station with a high school degree is more than 94%, and almost 60% have bachelor's degrees or higher. Compare this to Boston at 87.2% / 49.7% or Houston at 78.9% / 32.9%, and the difference becomes much more apparent.

This year TAMU is welcoming the single largest incoming freshman class of any university in our nation. Year after year, larger numbers of students dynamically affect the local population.

So, is the real estate market different in a college town? You bet it is. The youthfulness and highly educated population create a dynamic truly worthy of my investment of study and preparation required to assist in a sale or purchase.

College town differences for real estate sales

To help my sellers understand our market, we must first help them understand who is likely to purchase their house. Single-family homes are purchased primarily by two broad types and six sub-types of buyers.

Type A—The House Buyer would be the investment minded buyer.

Type B—The Home Buyer would be the long term "I want to raise my family in..." or "grow old in..." home buyer.

Type A
1. Investors wanting rental income
2. Parents wanting to minimize the 4–6 year cost of housing for their student

3. Highly paid business personnel brought in to partner with the school for 3-5 years

Type B

1. University instructional staff who may reside in the house 3-30 years

2. Returning former students who desire the college town's amenities

3. The general population

Each of these segments has different goals and timelines. One important factor the college town investor brings to our discussion is that they often do not live in the same town and instead employ a property management firm to maintain the property.

There are a high percentage of investment properties in a college town, typically located in the same neighborhoods where other segments reside. Student rentals have a direct (at least perceived) effect on the pricing of those neighborhoods and help to create what I call "micro-neighborhoods." A micro-neighborhood is a highly localized pocket of houses within an established neighborhood which is much smaller than the neighborhood itself with its own pricing. It can be as small as a cul-de-sac.

The Type A buyer is someone who knows they may only need the property for a short time. This buyer needs to be incredibly careful up front so they will not have regrets when trying to sell later.

Type A Investors find college towns very attractive. The return on investment has historically been above the average. This is due in part to the supply of affordable single-family homes available and the consistent demand for housing.

All markets experience fluctuation, but the consistent flood of new potential tenants—both young students and career professionals—makes the transient nature of a college town an extremely attractive investment market.

Our investors seek guidance to understand areas where a rental's success is most likely. We help them watch out for rental restrictions, tax appraisals, and the effects of micro-neighborhoods. My long-term investors who desire a great rate of return, consistent occupancy, and comparatively high rent rates are attracted to the opportunities in our college town. The key is purchasing correctly up front and knowing your long-term goals.

Parents of students are also investors. According to collegefactual.com it is projected that a freshman at TAMU in the fall of 2021 will be charged $82,324 for four years of on campus housing and dining. Also, this would *not* include the summer, and many residence halls require a move out even if you are staying during the summer. A student can certainly stay on campus and have everything provided for them in the dormitories—but where's the fun in that?

Parents who are purchasing a property for their student(s) recognize several advantages. For the student they see an opportunity to gain experience in property and relationship management. With the student in charge of the house they may need to collect the rent, pay the utility bills, and maintain the property. Many parents allow the student to collect the rents from roommates and keep all or a portion as spending money.

For the parents they realize the appreciation of value during the years of school and have an asset to sell at graduation possibly resulting in "no cost" housing. The significance of transforming an expense into a real investment with an increasing amount of equity which may be recovered after the 4-5 years of school is very appealing.

Families with multiple students looking to go to the same school, may see significant income from the off-campus investment. The potential savings or return on investment becomes even greater when you consider the potential tax write-offs on the investment property as well as the mortgage interest deduction currently available.

Incoming business professionals often have a healthy budget but know they must balance their "wants" with the reality that they may be leaving within a relatively short period of time. More time is usually your friend with real estate. Most of my business professional clients will make a conservative purchase knowing if their situation changes, they are in an excellent position to either move up within the area or out of the area as their company requests.

The Type B buyer is looking for just the right spot within their budget. They are more interested in the way the home "feels" and the long-term appeal of the area and proximity to the things they want to do.

Families will take the local schools, stores, and parks into great consideration. The professor may not be as concerned about local schools but will be quite budget conscious and look for a unique find that reflects his character. The returning former student is usually looking for something with great entertaining opportunities and is often looking in the high-end market.

While these are all overly broad generalizations, it is vital for the seller to understand where his property falls with regard to who will be interested in its purchase. Price entry point into the market is designed not only around comparable sales, the location, and the characteristics of the property, but also how it will appeal to the likely pool of potential buyers available.

Seasonal fluctuations

Another significant difference is the fluctuations of supply and demand based on season of the year—cycling regularly with the school year.

Before school starts, families compete with college parents who are looking for affordable housing for their students. Once school starts, these competing buyers usually pull out of the buying market.

I have often advised my single clients and young couples to watch the market but realize the better deals may come after the August start of school.

Another potential "deal" for fall buyers is from investors who were unable to lease their rental properties and want to sell since the house is likely to remain vacant until January or possibly the following August.

The must-knows

To be prepared as a seller, ask yourself these questions:

- Do I have the right information about my neighborhood?
- Do I know where my neighborhood truly begins and ends?
- Are there buying cycles in my neighborhood?
- Is my neighborhood more or less attractive to buyers than when I purchased?

- Within my neighborhood, are there forces working to change its character? For example, is the Homeowners' Association (HOA) easing up or becoming more restrictive? Does the market desire those changes?

- Can I get reliable data?

Like anyone who decides to sell their own house, sellers will ask and believe the neighbor who states they sold their 1970's style house in one day for the full asking price. This is rarely the full picture in any town. Texas is a non-disclosure state, meaning an owner is not compelled to share the actual sales price of his property. This is where my team shines. Our sellers know accurate data about the market as a whole and each micro-neighborhood specifically to make informed, intelligent decisions.

4 steps to selling in a college town

Selling (or buying) a home in a college town follows the same or similar steps as most other towns and must focus on the process of handling the vital listing activities. The beauty of this system is that you do not need an agent to work it.

Step 1: Uncover needs and prioritize

Is the timing of the sale the most important issue? Have you already accepted a job in another town and timing is essential? Or is the sales price the most important?

You may want to move up to a nicer house and need the most you can get to afford the purchase of the new house. These two needs often oppose each other. Knowing the market and how to position your house is essential.

Step 2: Staging and Photography

Staging your house to show on the real estate market is not interior design. Interior design is making a house more of a home. Staging is using the house itself as the best marketing tool you have. It is strategic placement of items to maximize the showing of the home. Your amazing property may not appear amazing to potential buyers unless you stage it well. The placement may not be practical for day-to-day living but accentuates the room to help buyers "see it" and its potential for them.

Step 3: Exposure

Homes sell due to two primary factors:

1. Price
2. Exposure

While the multiple list system (MLS) is the fastest way to the greatest exposure just about anywhere, in a small college town, word of mouth is still a key element. In this environment it's more likely to sell a property the "old fashioned way" by word of mouth. That can include one-on-one interactions, but also participation in small groups and organizations, both physically and virtually.

I frequently have quick conversations with other real estate agents who are seeking that "just right" property for their client. This kind of interaction with agents really does matter. One of my most recent sales was not found by the buyer through the MLS—instead, they saw it through one of my other advertising media and came directly to me.

Step 4: Negotiation

Negotiation is a balancing of priorities. So much can be lost at this point if the seller (or agent) did not invest appropriate time in Step 1. Money will be left on the table without the guiding balance of knowing/remembering the needs in the heat and emotion of the situation.

One of my sellers who is an engineering professor shared how grateful he was to have me involved. While he was certainly smart enough to handle the transaction alone, he appreciated my ability to plainly lay out the options before him as we chose whether to make counteroffers. He admitted I was right, there was more money he could ask for, but his wife wanted the security of knowing the deal was done. Understanding balance is critical and can even save your marriage!

Education can get in a seller's way

The education of the population in a college town is definitely a factor. Not only are the sellers well educated, but the buyers are also. A seller who does not take that into account may find himself in an undesirable situation without even realizing how he got there. Buyers often come in with unusual offers. The seller will need to be able to understand it clearly and unpack the twisted and confusing "pretzel" of information received in an offer.

The 4-step process outlined above is how to sell a house in any market. It is not rocket science, but I decided to make it my personal science and continue to study toward the mastery of it.

Sellers may understand how to sell their house, however, there is great value in having an ally with years of experience, and one who is intimately familiar with your market, to guide and handle the details for you. Merely knowing *how* to do something is different from knowing *how to do it well*. What I see in my smartest sellers is a tendency to over-analyze the situation. Remember to prioritize and stay focused on the most relevant issues and work to distinguish them from the interesting but non-relevant issues.

High- and low-end markets

The college affects a town's high-end areas indirectly. There are very few professors who earn hundreds of thousands of dollars each year. The high-end market effect comes instead from the managers and employees of the research partnerships brought to town. While academics drive the need for technology and infrastructure, it is the corporations with high earners and their high-quality talent that come to town due to the college as well as the retail and service providers who support them who purchase homes. Such high wage earners would not normally move to a small town, and thus push a higher-end buyer than we would normally see. The supply of high-end homes is often a smaller segment of a college-town market but is growing in my area.

Another driver in this top market tier comes from the former students who have climbed the corporate ladder and are now retiring. This segment knows what they want, and right now they are wanting to move back to their college towns. They're moving back for the sports, the culture, and the proximity to everything a university small town offers. The magnet of the college increases the area as a whole.

Yet another influence to the mid- to high-end market are parents who buy a larger house than the student needs to provide the parent a place to stay while in town. Many parents come for the football games or other events. College events are a huge influence and drive much of the local economy. Many parents and others converge on our town on game day weekends. Our local population will literally double each fall weekend when there is a home football game.

The low-end market is still present. Our economy is made up of all levels of earners and our low- to middle-income families love the area for the same reasons as the high-income families. Much of the lower end is made up of the oldest homes in the area.

Exceptions to this are the oldest properties closest to the school. In years past, investors purchased much of the oldest housing close to campus to maximize their investment. In the last 20 years, however, as buyers have begun to recognize and value homes with historic distinction, students and their parents do not want the "project" of an old house needing multiple upgrades. Those homes have instead been purchased by professors or retirees desiring a unique residence close to campus.

Upside even in a down market

In my time as a real estate agent in this college town, I have seen two downward turning markets nationwide. Nationally it was bad, but the college and its partnerships helped moderate our situation. During the 2008 great recession, the housing industry was hit horribly. However, thanks to a constant influx of students and parents needing to sell in our college town, the local ill effects of the economy's downturn were held off for nearly two full years.

The partnerships also helped maintain level incomes in the area, allowing our town time to adjust. That means our highs may rarely reach as high as the rest of the nation, but thankfully our lows are rarely as low either. During the recession, many new students came into the area to re-educate, and then stayed to continue the next level of education since jobs remained hard to find nationwide.

During that time, we saw our pricing take a hit. For several years, the normal appreciation was diminished or not present. While much of the nation saw a downturn in pricing and a massive loss of equity, there were only pockets in our market where we saw actual decreasing prices. Most of the pricing stayed constant—neither rising nor falling.

Sellers might bring cash to the closing table but only enough to cover the costs of selling. As an agent with access to the data, I was able to help my sellers understand how to position their home on the market to realize the greatest advantage. In our college town, real estate became the primary driver for local economic recovery.

Takeaways

As we evaluate college town real estate there are some important takeaways. Hyper-local knowledge is key to making the right investments as well as knowing how to price and even market a house for sale. The college town is a tale of two cities. One is a small town where just about everyone knows your name and the other is a metropolitan area with much bigger city amenities and personalities. The smalltown side rolls up the sidewalks at night and the Neighborhood Watch really is watching, while the metropolitan side has money and wants to burst at the seams with an event and activity list more like a city two to three times its size.

In summary, real estate in a small college town can be both challenging and confusing. My team excels at identifying pockets of interest and micro-neighborhoods helping navigate the zoning, favorable or unfavorable HOAs, as well as the new non-rental areas created by city ordinance. We know each investor, parent, buyer, or seller is unique; helping them calculate what they can do with real estate in our college town is what we do.

SELLING ON
YOUR IDEAL TIMELINE

WITH CHRISTINE SPARKS

Let's be clear—real estate takes an absurd amount of dedication to succeed and the hours are long and unpredictable. Oh, and let's not forget the competitiveness of the industry and **CHRISTINE SPARKS** thrives in this fast-paced, ever-changing environment. She is both passionate and highly skilled at helping clients navigate the decisions and choices necessary to complete a successful real estate transaction. Christine uses her boundless energy in conjunction with the latest technology and trends to her clients' advantage, handling the buying and selling of their properties with the utmost professionalism and skill.

At a personal level Christine is a wife to the sweetest and most patient man for over 20 years and the mother of three amazing (and mildly sarcastic) children. She holds degrees in both teaching (Lincoln Memorial University, TN) and Advertising Art (SUNY Farmingdale–Long Island, NY). She's an avid reader and active within her community. Real estate, with all its challenges, is simply another in a long line of successes for this young (ish?), hyper-motivated professional.

lovetoliveinknoxville.com
christinesparks@me.com
(865) 693-3232

SELLING ON
YOUR IDEAL TIMELINE

Generally speaking, do you need to sell before buying a new home? The answer is perhaps. Perhaps your financial circumstances dictate you must sell before you can buy or perhaps you just aren't comfortable buying before you sell. This is not the right solution for all but it is the right solution for some.

The decision is personal, but for a lot of people, buying before selling provides the comfort and flexibility they need.

Most believe they must sell before they can buy, but just the opposite can be shockingly beneficial. While it's not the best solution for everyone, it's worth a consideration to consider potential costs that could be avoided if you purchase before selling.

Not only are there some convenience and lifestyle circumstances where you might want to buy before selling but there financial benefits as well.

First, it increases the strength of your offer when you are submitting a bid on a property that is not contingent upon the sale of a current home. This affords you the opportunity to bargain on items such as price.

Second, you will have the time to find a home that best suits your needs. When you wait to buy until your home is already under contract, you might be scrambling to find your new home in weeks or sometimes days. This may force you to overlook aspects of a house that truly doesn't fit your search criteria because you are under the gun to lock in your next home fast.

Third, you will have the ability to consider homes that may need some updates or improvement—and often the potential for sweat equity.. This works especially well when there are special circumstance like a particular health concern, like making a home wheelchair accessible or converting to a no-threshold shower.

Lifestyle situations where it could be beneficial to buy before selling

- An older couple who has lived in a home for a long time is likely to own a lot of things. Downsizing and paring down belongings can take time.
- Families with school-aged children often want the kids to complete the school year before changing to another school.
- For families with homeschooled students or those with work-at-home careers, arranging times to show their home to potential buyers is challenging.
- When there are health concerns in the home, day-to-day caregiving can make showings almost impossible.

How to do it

If you have fully paid down your mortgage, it's a clear-cut process. If you still carry a balance on your current mortgage, typically you must be able to carry both mortgages (the principal, interest, taxes, and insurance—PITI—on your current home, *plus* PITI for the new home).

These programs are called "recasting," "delayed down payment" or sometimes they are offered as a portfolio product or in-house program, if you qualify.

Borrowers are required to put down 5% toward the purchase of the new home. Once the current home sells, they can apply those net proceeds to the new loan. The lender, for a small fee, will recast the remaining loan balance, after applying the net proceeds, or a portion thereof, over the remaining term of the loan.

Example:

- $500,000 new loan amount on a 30-year term (360 months)

- Re-Cast: $100,000 in net proceeds applied to the principal balance of the new loan perhaps 3 months later

- New Loan: $400,000 recast over the remaining term (in this example, 357 months) which essentially lowers the monthly payment to what it would have been if the borrowers had the $100k at the time of closing 3 months prior

Generally speaking, the fee to recast is $350-600, depending on the service provider, which is obviously much less than refinancing after purchase to apply the curtailment.

*** It is important to note this is different than a bridge loan. Consult a qualified mortgage professional for guidance.*

Getting started

Okay, so you have decided this is the best route for you and your family. Where do you begin?

Here is a sneak peek into our 4-step process. It is slow and methodical in preparation and planning so you can be quick at the end when the magic happens.

Step 1: Staging
Months before you are ready to purchase, formulate a plan to prep your home for the eventual sale. Have a stager come out and provide a consultation. Recommendations can include repairs or updates needed, paring down extra furniture or basement/attic items, painting, etc. Quotes and estimates are obtained and the work is scheduled.

Marketing prep includes scheduling professional photos, completing a home-tour video, creating feature sheets, and all print and media marketing.

Step 2: Financing
Get your financing approved. Numbers are everything. Wanting a new home is fantastic but it's all about the numbers. I always estimate a sales price conservatively, because I want you to work from a worst-case scenario— even though I'm always going to sell your property for a much higher price... but then it's just gravy. ☺

Step 3: Buying
Then we go to the buy-side and find a home that is the perfect fit for you. When you get excited about moving to a new home, it can be emotional. That's the beautiful thing that happens when you discover a house you love.

Step 4: Selling
Immediately after you complete home inspections on the new property and know you're moving forward, then place your current home on the market. Since you proactively completed the pre-marketing at the beginning of the

process, generally speaking, your home can be sold within the first few days.

Most of the time, before I help clients even start looking, we talk and make sure they qualify to carry both homes. We also develop a what-if contingency plan, but my goal is for you to not ever have to use it.

Prior to finding your next home we get everything prepped and ready to go on your sell-side so we can focus on finding your dream home. Then immediately, once you've got the new property under contract, we start marketing the home you currently live in.

Our goal is to almost simultaneously, or very shortly after you move, close the sale on your current home. In that case, since you get that first month of mortgage free, you may never actually carry two mortgages.

Skills to look for in a Realtor

You need to look for a real estate agent who legitimately has a plan and vendor relationships that can offer the types of products you will need—home stagers, decluttering consultations, contractors for repairs, professional photography, and marketing. Making sure your home is prepped for speedy sale is the most important part of the process.

The best agents also have an in-house staff that specializes in your selling situation and also understands your buying situation. Together they can manage not just the marketing and sales of those two properties, but also your personal timeline of repairs, moving, and closing funds. There are lots of moving parts in this process!

Making everyone happy

I worked with the Bensons off and on for years. The husband wanted waterfront property but the wife hated water and wanted acreage. It was important to each of them that the other was happy, so we would bounce back and forth, never quite finding something they both liked.

Then we stumbled upon a waterfront property that was on a couple of acres. It was the right amount of land and the ideal location, but the wife hated the actual house.

In frustration, they started thinking about buying an empty lot and building a new home. It was killing me. I could see the potential for the waterfront property on the acreage. The property had a gentle slope to the water, with year-round deep water looking out onto the main channel. It was absolutely breathtaking.

We scheduled an appointment with one of my design consultants who was able to help the couple meld a vision of what the home could become after renovation. We were able to show them how they could make this the home of their dreams while they stayed in their current home.

During the consultation we:
- Developed an understanding of the clients' aesthetic
- Analyzed their budget goals and confirmed the had sufficient funds for the remodel
- Brought in trusted contractors and vendors to ensure the remodel could be completed within the required timeframe.

We determined all the changes that both the husband and wife wanted could be made within their timeframe... while also staying within their budget. It was all systems go on the dream house! Time to focus on their current home.

Together we created a plan. They preferred to wait to list their home until the remodel was mostly complete. However, we didn't want to wait until the last minute and risk missing the opportunity to get top dollar for their current home. Knowing market conditions can change in the blink of an eye, we agreed to check in periodically.

Thankfully all the metrics indicated it was a seller's market, and in fact inventory was reaching record lows. It was *prime* condition to sell, plus they'd had the benefit of buying before the market values rose. It was the perfect scenario.

Approximately one month prior to completion of the remodel, we listed their house kicked our marketing into high gear. We focused on the home's unique features, specifically the pool and outdoor pavilion and kitchen. The backyard was divine and we played off scarcity and created a bidding war.

Because of our propriety marketing plan, guaranteeing we would sell their home over the average price in under the average days—*drama free*—their home sold for more than any other in that neighborhood. Our prelisting marketing plan created an auction-like experience.

The couple was able to enjoy their existing home until the moment their remodel was completed, knowing we would get their home sold when the time was right for them. Our team stayed in contact throughout the renovation process, constantly monitoring the market for changes, and assessing the right time to list.

The end result was the stuff of dreams—the kind of stuff other agents without the experience and connections tell you can't be done. The Bensons were able to procure their dream home, tailor it to their personal needs and aesthetic, and then wait to move in until after the remodel so they never had to live in a construction zone. Oh, and they sold for top dollar!

Reasons to work with us

If the idea of buying before you sell sounds appealing and you would like to discuss further, give us a call! This is just a small portion of our home-selling process. We create a customized plan tailored to your needs.

It's often better to buy before you sell and this process can works seamlessly for you. Finding an agent who fights to find a creative solution for you and has proven track record of success doesn't have to be hard. One thing is always the same—take it slowly on the front end to speed things up on the back end.

Whether you buy before you sell or after, we are able to create a marketing plan that gets you above-average price in below-average time—*drama free.*

SELLING YOUR DESTINATION HOME TO OUT-OF-TOWN BUYERS

WITH GARRETT & DONNA SANDELL

GARRETT and **DONNA SANDELL** are from a small town in South Central Kansas at the edge of Flint Hills, Winfield, Kansas. They grew up in the surrounding area and raised their families there. Donna has sold real estate since 1993 and Garrett worked in the automotive industry. They love the sunshine and "Salt Life" lifestyle and were frequently drawn to Florida.

Garrett and Donna joined Keller Williams in 2013 and service the Marco Island/Naples areas. They enjoy meeting new people from all over the world and helping them discover everything that Southwest Florida has to offer. They work together to prepare and guide you through the buying and selling process, as well as help you navigate and disseminate the overwhelming amount of information. They strive to be the pinnacle of a great customer experience.

Their mission is to educate, inform and serve.
—"Livin' the Dream Team"

www.teamsandellswfl.com
teamsandellswfl@gmail.com
(239) 682-7600

SELLING YOUR DESTINATION HOME TO OUT-OF-TOWN BUYERS

When selling a destination property to an out-of-town buyer, the first distinction is that quality professional photography is an absolute must, including video. Because over 96% of home buyers start their search on the internet these days, your prospective buyers will begin searching online, sometimes months in advance of their trip to visit the property. Due to the 2020 pandemic and continuing into 2021, a lot of showings are now virtual-only.

You want to create a feeling of "presence" for your home, online, that someone would feel during an in-person visit. You want the home to really pop and stand out.

For years now, we've had a 5-point system for identifying ideal buyers outside of the local market, to maximize value for destination sellers. We email your home listing to our database of thousands of home buyers all across the globe, as well as post it to hundreds of websites. In today's world, numerous social media sites are also a must. These recommendations are based on our system that we've been successfully running for years.

Working with an out-of-town buyer

You have to paint the picture for them because the out-of-town buyer is not physically at your home. In addition to the exterior and interior of the property, you also need to talk about its location. Since we're on an island and most folks have a boat in the canal or bay behind their homes, we talk about distance from the dock to the Gulf. Sun exposure on the pool is important as well. People come for our sunshine and warm weather so they want to maximize both.

When someone is viewing your destination home online, you can't just meet with them in ten minutes and walk around the property. Instead, you can create virtual showings, inside and out—physically showing the property via streaming video like you would if the buyer were there in person.

Selling to an out-of-town buyer requires an advanced use of technology that brings with it an entire world of opportunities. You can offer a detailed walk-through of the property, answering buyer questions as they come up.

In addition to the visual elements of your house, you can talk about key selling points of your home and unique community. When well done, this tool can actually elicit buyers to make an offer, subject to in-person viewing before closing, or going ahead and purchasing without having been there themselves.

The amazing tech that makes it possible

FaceTime, Google Duo, and Zoom are tools we use to walk buyers through your home. When you can offer same-day showings through virtual technology, you get real-time feedback and help buyers narrow their criteria for a faster and smoother buying experience.

You can also use technology to help buyers obtain local financing, coordinate on-site inspections, appraisals, surveys, and other essential services even when they may be hundreds or thousands of miles away.

We can help find stagers for sellers or decorators for buyers, so the home will be fabulous whenever needed. When working with an out-of-area buyer, there are some challenges, but also major opportunities. Working with the right agent and the right system will incorporate these technologies to allow someone thousands of miles away to find their island paradise.

Finding the biggest audience

On Marco Island, as with many second-home markets, one of the hot spots is turnkey furnished properties. This means the buyer purchases not only the house, but also all the furnishings and decorations that make it possible for them to immediately be able to use their vacation home.

With this in mind, it's important for your home to be staged and furnished properly, with the latest and greatest. It doesn't have to be the most expensive, but, for example, a beach property should feature beautiful, clean and fresh coastal-style furnishings. That way your buyer can imagine themselves ready to walk in, needing only their toothbrush and a pair of flip-flops.

Either you as the seller can prepare and stage your home, or you can find a great agent who will prepare it for you. Bear in mind that you will be showing off the home through pictures and videos. Certain homes may have a terrific feel when visited on-site, but if they're not prepped well for photo and video, they can actually look worse on the internet or on a virtual walk-through. Think about the way light is reflected and absorbed. Also think about camera angles that will highlight the openness and availability of the rooms, rather than making them feel tight and constricted. In fact, when marketing to out-of-area buyers, camera angles are the equivalent of the smell and feel of an in-person visit.

In our market of Marco Island, Florida, the furniture and decor allows buyers to feel the energy of the island culture. It communicates a recreational second-home feel... suitcase ready!

Timing for out-of-market buyers

Consider the seasonality of your home. Here in Florida, we're definitely more of a snowbird market. Properties get the most eyes from January 1st through March 31st and with virtual work now available to more people, our season is getting longer.

You want to make your home readily available during those peak times of year. Investors do well with our rental market, so sometimes a home or condo is rented and unavailable for in-person showings. In such a case, it is imperative to have great pictures, a virtual online tour, and floor plans available for buyers.

In our market, summer is getting busier with folks from the southern U.S. taking advantage of our beaches, fishing, and the Everglades for family vacations.

From our experience, however, we can testify that some of the most successful, serious buyers will visit out-of-season. They want to look when properties are more available and easier to get under contract quickly. Many times this results in higher and more qualified offers.

There's a difference between impulsive buyers and prepared buyers. Destination sellers understand the need to attract out-of-area buyers as well as the seasonality of the market.

A mountain town is going to be different than a seaside town, but in either location, you can benefit from having a world-class local real estate expert on your team—someone who understands that peak seasons for tourists might be different than for buyers.

For example, in our Marco Island pre-season, we spend time talking to buyers in the early fall as they prepare to escape the Northern winters. They want to plan ahead so they are set up to go South when the winter chill sets in. Seasoned buyers tend to be prepared, know the island and Naples area well, and already have their favorite spots. They know what island location they want, or their favorite area of Naples, and can easily make a fast decision.

Both kinds of buyers are important. There is no right or wrong. They're just different. When you become aware of these differences, or work with an agent who understands both buyer groups, you'll learn to communicate to them in the way that will be most effective.

The impulsive buyer wants to fill a need or a dream right now, while the prepared buyer wants to take advantage of time and planning to locate their dream destination home.

After a phone consultation, we can usually recommend the perfect locale for that buyer based on their criteria, hobbies, and family needs. It may be a gated community with all the finest amenities or on the island with a magnificent bay or beach view. Either way, we are here to guide customers through the process.

Success story

Snowbirds Dean and Kate walked into our office looking for an agent, and we found them their vacation home so they could enjoy frequent trips south from the bitter cold of

Northeast winters. They have since become our friends, and recently they were looking for another gorgeous new home. When one caught their eye, Garrett made a quick trip out to meet them and walk through the property. They put it under contract that day.

We quickly listed their current property in a popular resort-style subdivision with golf courses, and went to work. Using our techniques outlined above, we set the neighborhood record on the sale of Dean and Kate's picture-perfect home.

Their neighbors, Tom and Sue, were naturally curious about the record-breaking sale, so Dean and Kate referred their friends to us. They obviously came to us with high expectations!

Tom and Sue's home was tastefully decorated and a great place to spend the winters. You could hardly even tell they lived there. But at this point in their lives, they were drawn to the crystal shores and pristine beach on Marco Island where they found themselves frequenting favorite restaurants and happy hour spots. We quickly listed and sold their home in the same resort subdivision for another record-setting price and set out to find their perfect beach home.

Garrett watched the local MLS with hawk-like eyes. One day, there it was. With killer one-of-a-kind views in a unique gated community right on the beach, this place had it all—restaurants, executive golf course, golf cart paths, etc.

We called them on FaceTime immediately, because we knew this view wouldn't last long in our market. Tom and Sue took our advice and made an offer right away. Success! The home was theirs. Our knowledge of the market and their trust in us made it happen quickly or it would have been gone.

They love their new beach home and we were so happy to help them find their perfect destination spot.

We feel fortunate to do what we love in a beautiful place while making new friends at the same time. We get to spend our days working together, helping customers find their paradise. It's so rewarding. And then, we go join new and old friends for happy hour! What could be better? We feel very blessed.

SELLING YOUR HOME FOR ABSOLUTE TOP DOLLAR

WITH DAVID VANASSCHE

As a seasoned real estate professional, **DAVID VANASSCHE** recognizes and values the trust clients place in him and his team and his work toward the goal of exceeding their expectations.

He has consistently trained new agents into highly effective professionals by leading, guiding, and equipping them with the tools, training, and support needed to allow them to deliver world-class value and results.

Outside of real estate, David enjoys contributing to the community by serving as a sports official, officiating high school wrestling and networking with other small businesses in the area through on-camera interviews with his YouTube channel, *Spotlight on the Valley.*

David VanAssche and his team, The VanAssche Group, are based in Phoenix, AZ, with additional offices in Scottsdale and Chandler.

www.phoenixareahome.com
david@thevanasschegroup.com
(480) 588-8288

SELLING YOUR HOME FOR ABSOLUTE TOP DOLLAR

Like a professional athlete who practices the same plays over and over again, the fundamentals of throwing or catching a football never change, regardless of the weather, or the team that is being played against. Expertise allows fine adjustments and in-the-moment decisions to take place along the way, but the fundamentals remain the same, and are highly trained for.

This is also true in real estate. Top-performing agents—those who repeatedly and predictably deliver desirable results to their clients—follow the same process each time, making only small adjustments as required by the situation at hand. The under-the-surface, core fundamentals that have been practiced and fine-tuned never change. These top-performing agents, like pro-athletes, have an entire team of professionals behind them that allow them to perform and deliver at peak level.

What stands in the way?

The problem in real estate is that more than 90% of agents expect to be paid like professional athletes, yet only train and support at the "Parks & Rec" level. Another problem in real estate is that the public has been led to believe that a professional-level agent is generally worth the same compensation as a brand new agent who is "taking a stab" at their first home sale.

Most agents in the industry simply do not have established processes, systems, tools, and go-to resources. Most are literally "winging it" and their actions are dramatically affecting the outcome of their client's experience—and the bottom-line dollars their client will walk away with from the transaction.

> *Sad fact:* 87% of real estate agents fail out of the business within two years of starting. It's upsetting to know that the small handful of clients they worked with during their short tenures—clients who probably paid professional-athlete level fees— most certainly received only Parks & Rec level service and results.

How do you choose?

When it comes to hiring an agent to sell your home, do you choose your spouse's boss's nephew because you want to "throw him a bone" and help him out, or do you interview multiple top agents to learn who you believe has the best systems, processes, team members, assistants, vendor partners, and a track record of proven success?

That person will ultimately be the agent you believe is equipped to lead and guide you and the situation to the smoothest and most desirable outcome. But how can you decide?

We believe the fundamentals of selling for absolute top dollar, in any market, follow a logical, repeatable process. Top agents are experts at the implementation and execution of a well devised sales process, and can make on-the-fly adjustments to fit any situation along the way.

The plan starts with identifying the ideal buyer for your property. Frankly, in most cases the ideal buyer is someone who has money to spend and does not want drama. We're usually not interested in selling to investors, flippers, or iBuyers. The best systems, processes, and plans attract the best buyers.

Our 3-stage, 7-step plan

Here's how we sell a home at top dollar:

Stage 1

Positioning—Getting Your Home "Ready for Market"

Step 1: Pre-Inspection

> The auto industry has repeatedly proven that the public will pay more for a "pre-owned, pre-certified" Honda Civic at the dealership than they will for the exact same car from some guy on Craigslist or Facebook.
>
> A pre-inspected home by a licensed third-party home inspector, including a report (documenting any repairs made before listing for sale) available to buyers as a marketing document will dramatically increase the perceived and actual value of what a buyer is willing to pay.
>
> This assurance will make them more comfortable and confident in what they are buying. Risk of surprises will always cast doubt, and cause a buyer who is willing to pay the highest price to mentally limit the amount they might otherwise spend if fear or objections were already addressed.

Step 2: Home Staging

> Staging is very different than interior design. Interior designers design the layout of the home, paint colors,

and furniture to suit the individual people who will be living in the house. Home stagers, on the other hand, design the layout of the home to appeal to the widest possible audience, advising which furniture should remain in the home, where it should be placed, and if any minor improvements such as paint or carpet replacement should be done to maximize the look and feel for someone who will *never* sit down in the home... rather walking through it for about 12 minutes before they decide to write an offer of purchase. This approach and mindset is critically important and easily overlooked by part-time, inexperienced, or poorly trained agents.

Step 3: Professional Photos

The first showing of your home happens online. Buyers make split-second decisions on whether they intend to see the home (or buy it remotely) within seconds of swiping through photos on their mobile device. Visit any real estate website and you'll quickly find listings with the *worst* photos imaginable. Having high-quality photos from a professional photographer is mandatory when you want to sell your property for top dollar. (Hint: Most agents are not professional picture-takers and "cheap out" with their iPhone.)

Stage 2
Marketing & Communications

Step 4: Identifying Niches

What is it about your home that is special and unique? What would catch a buyer's attention that would lock their sights on your home over a competing property? Clearly identifying all of the special and unique characteristics of your home, the block, the neighborhood, and the town or city will be critical to the marketing and communication strategy used to attract buyers, take attention away from competing homes, and obtain strong offers.

Step 5: Creating Scarcity

A major aspect of a good communication strategy is creating scarcity. For example when someone says, "Tell us about the house," the answer given can be as basic (and unfortunately, typical) of "We're selling a 4-bed, 2.5-bath home on a quarter-acre. Would you like to see it?"

A more professional strategy to create scarcity is to frame the response more like, "We're selling a home with an amazing garden containing multiple fruiting trees and an automatic watering system. The attached garage has oversized bays to make it easy to park a full-size SUV or pickup truck. Inside, the kitchen was just recently updated with all stainless-steel appliances. Would you like to see it?"

Creating scarcity in the mind of the buyer—pointing out the things they may (or may not!) be able to find in a competing property—will compel them to see it, which is critical to maximizing the number of eyeballs on the property.

Step 6: Creating Urgency

Making big purchases can always bring doubt and frustration. Communication surrounding the creation of urgency to compel a buyer to take action (and make an offer) are varied and many.

Common examples might include: scheduling showings back-to-back to ensure buyers see each other coming and going, or putting pressure on a buyer to see the home today (Wednesday) rather than this weekend because "We're expecting offers and it might not last till the weekend."

Communication around urgency is a practiced skill and an expert will properly utilize this powerful tool to your advantage.

Stage 3

Negotiation

Step 7: Negotiation

This is what all the planning, preparation, and expert execution leads to—negotiating an offer. It's been said that by the time a buyer writes their offer, more than 80% of the negotiation is already over. The powerful thing about negotiation is that it doesn't begin with the writing of a contract... it begins from the very first contact with a potential buyer.

Expert real estate professionals are intentional and strategic from the beginning in how they position a home, market the home, communicate with potential buyers, create scarcity and urgency in the mind of a buyer, and lead them to the offer.

Ideally, we want multiple buyers (or a lingering "threat" of multiple buyers) to weigh heavily on the person who will ultimately buy the home. We want that buyer to become emotionally attached to the property, be confident in the condition, and be comfortable (and even excited or proud) about paying top dollar for the home.

None of this happens by accident! Those long-range passes, dramatic touchdowns, and 40-yard field goals are the result of consistent and expert preparation. The same is true of what you can expect from top real estate agents with the constantly trained skills, systems, and expertise to confidently and consistently land you in the most desirable position.

If you happen to be in the Phoenix, AZ area, call us. If you're looking for an agent in another area of the country, call us and we'll introduce you to someone in your area who will do a phenomenal job!

SELLING & BUYING
IN ONE SMOOTH MOVE

WITH LESLIE STEWART

LESLIE STEWART was born and raised in Las Vegas, and has witnessed the extreme changes in the real estate market over the years. A product of the Clark County School District, she is a graduate of the original Las Vegas High School downtown campus and earned her degree from the University of Nevada, Las Vegas, in real estate. This city is Leslie's home, and she has worked to help others find their homes for over a decade. In fact, she is among the top 5% of real estate agents in the valley.

When buying a home, she zones in on the details of her client's needs, stays in constant communication, and leverages her vast network to find the perfect home. Her negotiating skill when submitting offers has a winning track record when there are multiple offers. Sellers know her experience will help them sell their home quickly and hassle-free. The Stewart Team has a process to help sellers prepare their homes for sale, resulting in offers above the average price and in less time than the industry standard. More than a job, real estate is her passion.

Leslie and her husband of 25 years are both natives of Las Vegas and have four children and two mini Dachshunds. She is an active member of her church and the Scottish Celtic community. She currently serves on the board for the Las Vegas Highland Dance Association and the Las Vegas Pipe Band.

www.stewartlvrealestate.com
leslie@stewartlvrealestate.com
(702) 526-3404

SELLING & BUYING
IN ONE SMOOTH MOVE

You can't escape it... people are always moving and curious to know what their neighbor's home sold for, how much their own home is worth, and what would it take to purchase their dream home.

First-time home buyers who are looking to graduate into the buy/sell arena have a related question: "How can we buy and sell a home at the same time?" They are usually confident they can sell but worried they can't buy, or confident they can buy the perfect home but feel they are not able to sell their current residence.

The best way to start this journey is to connect with a real estate professional and have a conversation that will liberate you from false challenges that may have paralyzed you with fear. A highly skilled agent should be doing more asking and listening, than telling and showing. A great agent will understand your timeline, your financial situation, and help you create your personalized strategy to reach your goals.

Knowing how to navigate this process is imperative. A lot of buyers, sellers, and real estate agents make the big mistake of rushing out to look at houses or putting a sign in the yard before they have a strategy mapped out. They haven't thought through what's most important. The homeowners may have an end goal in sight, but there are multiple paths to be explored to ensure the correct one is being forged.

Market temperature

Once you have established your ideal path, an agent will start working on the logistical portion of the plan to confirm it can become reality. It is important that everyone knows the temperature of your current market and factors that into your strategy. You will receive an estimate on what price you can expect your current residence to sell for and a realistic range of how much money you will have to apply to the purchase of your new home.

Your agent will connect you with a reputable lender who has experience with buyer/seller client needs and who can work on your prequalification. This lender will also have some exploratory conversations in regard to the current financial picture and discuss options like what type of loan is best, how much down payment is needed, if you can carry both mortgages, or if your purchase will be contingent on the sale of your current residence.

It's so important to understand your numbers before you go out and fall in love with that dreamy kitchen or backyard with a pool!

In any city there are price differences depending on the location. This is true for the city of Las Vegas and its suburb of Henderson. Regardless of where you are, you might decide to explore options that fit into your budget better or in a less competitive area.

We want to set you up for success, finding your next dream home—within your means—especially if it's a situation where your purchase is contingent on selling your current home. Whether it's location or price point, you have an opportunity to enjoy your home and create wealth.

Expectations

Now that the purpose has been defined and the logistics have commenced, we are moving into the action portion of our strategy and this is where you need mental and physical strength.

Setting the right expectations is not a perfect science, but by working together, you and your agent can eliminate as many uncertainties as possible on the front end, although you will still need to have some flexibility to reach your end goal.

There is more strength in flexibility—like a skyscraper. Skyscrapers are built to withstand strong winds by having some give. A flexible skyscraper reduces stress at the joints which makes them stronger and less prone to collapse. Similar to a skyscraper, once we understand nothing is linear and build in flexibility we can create the blueprint of your real estate plan.

Equally important is understanding factors outside of our control, like price elasticity. The value of a home you are going to sell and the value of a home you really want to buy may truly shift every day. The market is constantly fluctuating. When a neighbor's house sells, the comps change. Interest in a neighborhood changes based on what happens within the school districts and zoning. Plus, things like, a change of HOA management, the building of new retail or restaurants, or ownership change of certain parcels could have an impact on the value of any property.

You need to remain flexible, and recognize the market is always moving. Emotions are heightened when dealing with real estate because it is the foundation of family and security. It is also typically your largest asset and investment. When uncertainties start to crop up, sometimes we make decisions based on emotions rather than logic. The key point is to remember your original goals, and to manage expectations.

Sellers tend to be more analytical, and buyers tend to be more emotional, but when you're both a seller and a buyer, that means there are going to be ups and downs as well as swings. Maintaining a clear vision constantly can give you the upper hand when the challenges come.

For example, you may receive a less than desirable offer and be offended by it. Don't be. Another way to view this is as a power play—you have an offer in hand and that can propel potential offers to higher than anticipated prices.

The prep

Now that you understand the importance of being flexible and mentally strong, we want to take a look at the physical activities and strategy built around selling and buying at the same time.

Preparing a home to sell can be overwhelming, but if there is a proven strategy implemented there is no need to fear. Utilizing strategy gives control to the sellers and eliminates unknowns for you and your future buyer.

Complete a home inspection beforehand, and then you have control in mitigating repairs. Next comes staging your home to attract the most buyers and validates value. Follow up with professional photography and videography, and most importantly, price your home competitively compared to its appraised value and competition currently on the market.

Eliminating one of these steps can set the transaction back, causing the timeline and plan to need to be readjusted. I worked with a client who needed to sell and buy, but he struggled with the definition and purpose of staging. He did not fully understand the process and, unfortunately, this meant his house stood on the market for longer than desired. Once he realized he omitted a vital step of the process, and the stager was able to pare down on his personal belongings and rearrange the home to open the living space. After fully committing to this plan he received a full-price offer within a week.

Staging was a hidden gem to this client who was downsizing from a two-story home to a one-story home. By adding this step, it helped him when he received that full-price offer with a request for a quick close.

All these little factors compound to create a quicker sale, so you can have the strength when it's time to put in your offer. We go through each of these steps and prepare ahead so that when the seller or seller's agent of the home you want to purchase on contingency asks, we can show them something compelling, unlike those without a strategic plan. They will immediately understand your home is going to sell quickly, and for top dollar, which makes you a really low-risk buyer.

When your current home generates a large pool of buyers to choose from, with multiple offers, if something falls through with one buyer, then you have other offers to fall back on. Strategically it makes the offer you're placing on your new dream home all that much stronger.

Timing

When the purchase of your dream home is contingent on the sale of your current residence, we have to close on your current home first. Sometimes it can be done on the same day as closing on your new home, and for others there are a couple of days or weeks in between.

There are endless options to stage your transition, possibly leasing it back for a couple of weeks or renting a POD to hold non-essentials while closing on the second house. Sometimes those who need to sell and buy at the same time stay with friends or family for a short period of time, or even an Airbnb or other short-term rental.

A good agent will help you make sure you have the best possibilities planned out ahead of time. To ensure your sales transaction works out really well, it may be worth a week or two in an extended-stay hotel. With the right system in place, you will never end up homeless! After 10+ years in the business, I've never had someone legitimately need to go find a place to stay.

A large component to the success on this process is defining and being very aware of the contractual timelines. Typically, on the sale of a home with a mortgage, you're looking at a 30- to 45-day timeframe. But if your financing will only let you carry one mortgage, then we need to sell your current home first before we can close on the new home. In this case, you may be looking at more of a 60-day timeframe.

In the case of new construction, the timing all comes down to the builder. From start to finish, it could be a good nine months until you can move into that property. In a seller-leaning market we are seeing owners able to negotiate a leaseback to ensure only moving once.

This is exactly what we were able to negotiate for a family this year. This couple had been trying to buy and sell for two years. They entered the process with a lot of fear and concern about selling their home without having one ready to buy that they really loved.

We went through the process and got their home totally ready to sell. They quickly found a house that they were interested in, and we submitted an offer. Their offer was accepted despite it being contingent upon the sale of their home, because we had everything ready to go, to list their current home the next day. Due to the prep work we had done, we dominated and created the optimum opportunity for them, including a lease back, in addition to more money so they could make improvements and move into the turnkey property they were dreaming of.

Don't let fear stop you from fulfilling your vision of moving into your dream home. Yes, there are a lot of moving pieces to juggle, and it can easily get overwhelming. Working with a real estate agent who has expertise in this area will remove stress and make this journey as seamless as possible. With the right strategy the unknowns of doing a simultaneous buy/sell are overcome and you won't end up homeless or needing to move twice.

NEGOTIATING FOR RECORD-BREAKING SALES PRICES

WITH JOHN KANICKA & JEREMY PAYNE

The Todd Tramonte Home Selling team is full of former athletes, but none are quite like **JOHN KANICKA**. A marketing specialist in Dallas-Fort Worth, John has a background as a competitive figure skater, competing professionally on an international level for four years. In 1997, he took silver in the U.S Open Professional Championships. The following year, he placed seventh in the World Professional Figure Skating Championships held in Jaca, Spain. He brings that same competitive drive to his career, and it shows up most clearly with how he aggressively negotiates on behalf of his clients to put thousands of extra dollars into their pockets.

He also applies his background from coaching figure skating to help counsel clients through the process of selling their home. His leadership inspires confidence and brings clarity to his clients as they work together to sell their home. His heart for coaching also comes out when he has the chance to help other team members. John goes the extra mile for his teammates and clients alike.

At the top of his priority list are his children: Autumn (20), Paris (18), and Gabe (15). Whether it's driving to dance lessons, coaching sports teams, or building sets for plays, if his kids are involved in it, John is involved in it. He is engaged to his fiancée Liz. They enjoy living in Dallas, where John has resided for over 20 years, for the city's great restaurants, parks and golf courses.

www.dallashomerealty.com
john@toddtramonte.com
(972) 632-0630

JEREMY PAYNE serves as a marketing specialist on the Todd Tramonte Home Selling Team in Dallas-Fort Worth. Jeremy uses his natural gifts of influence, communication and strategic negotiation to act as a consultant solely for sellers in his market, and execute his team's Over/Under marketing system.

You won't meet a more competitive person than Jeremy, which becomes an invaluable asset when his goal is to break home sales records and make his clients tens of thousands of dollars more than they would with a different agent. His first two years as a Marketing Specialist on the team, he personally led clients through $32M in home sales, and is on pace to sell well over $20M in his third year. He has also won his brokerage's "Home Run Agent" award 15 out of the first 28 months it's been given, an award given to that month's top-producing agent. But the most impressive part is the fact that his clients' home sales are currently averaging over 13% above what other homes are selling for in each of those neighborhoods. He is proud to be a part of a team that is able to distinguish itself by having a tangible impact on the lives of their clients through their real estate transaction.

Jeremy grew up visiting family in DFW, so he and wife Jen were excited to move to the area shortly after graduating from Texas A&M University in 2012 and getting married in 2013. They currently reside in Plano. Jeremy and Jen have three children. After having two sons, Hudson and Cooper, they had their first daughter, Avery, in August 2020.

In his free time, Jeremy is an avid golfer. His recent achievement was pulling off the rare feat of an albatross—shooting 3-under-par on a par-5 hole. He is also heavily invested in his church, CityBridge Community Church in Plano, where he plays bass guitar in the worship band.

www.dallashomerealty.com
jeremy@toddtramonte.com
(972) 269-5074

NEGOTIATING FOR RECORD-BREAKING SALES PRICES

The National Association of Realtors does frequent research on consumer behavior. Nearly every year in recent history, the data shows that the #1 reason homeowners hire real estate agents to sell their home is for expertise in negotiation.

This makes sense. What does not make sense however is that in nearly every state in the United States, the state portion of the real estate licensing educational requirements and the state licensing exam require exactly zero courses about negotiating. The national portion of the education and exam also requires not one single hour of negotiation training.

We are embarrassed on behalf of our entire industry that after years of clear and compelling logic, this is still the case. Millions of real estate agents are kind, well-intentioned neighbors who want to be great. But most simply are not.

What is negotiation?

If you want to negotiate record-breaking prices, repair amendments and non-realty items when selling your home, you'll want to follow the 3-part approach laid out in this chapter, or you'll want a full-time, dedicated, world-class real estate agent and negotiator on your side who does.

When most people hear the word "negotiating," they usually think of haggling over the terms of the contract. If a home is listed at $300k and an offer comes in at $280k, it typically means the seller will make a counter-offer to come down to $295k and the buyer will respond by coming up to $285k, then the two parties will meet in the middle at $290k.

But that's not what we mean when we talk about negotiation. There is an actual skill and proficiency that has nothing to do with haggling.

We define negotiation differently—anything that affects your time, stress, or money throughout the process of selling your home.

Money is naturally a major factor, but time and stress are often overlooked. Yet they are usually big factors to a seller and can be what determines the positive or negative emotions the seller remembers years down the road.

Let's say the property goes on the market on a Friday. On Saturday morning an agent calls and says, "Hey, is the property on Main Street still available, and are you working any offers? What can you tell me about it?"

Most agents in the industry would reply, "It's a great house... 3-bedroom, 2-bath. It has 2,000 square feet. Um no, we don't have any offers yet, but we'd love to work with you guys. The sellers are super motivated. Let me know if you have any other questions."

That's a pretty standard call, but truthfully, sometimes the agent doesn't even answer the phone, and if they do, they don't have that much information in front of them, so they say, "Let me call you back." And then it leads to nothing.

If you role play that out, let's say their buyers visit the house that Saturday for a tour. They really like it. At the end, they go out to the front yard and say, "Hey, Mr. Agent. We think this is the one. We absolutely love this house. Do you think it's priced well? Should we make an offer, and if so, where should we come in?"

What is that agent likely to say? "Well, I talked with the listing agent yesterday and he said they didn't have any offers yet. It is a beautiful home, but he didn't really have much to give me other than what's already online. But he did say that the sellers were super motivated."

This scenario sets the buyers up to feel like they have the most leverage in negotiations. It also makes them more likely to submit a low-ball offer. "Let's try and get them to come down. Then we play the meeting-in-the-middle game, which is what happens in almost every transaction."

Now let's change that original phone call.

Let's say a buyer agent calls and instead hears, "Hey, make sure you write this down. This is a one of a kind home - it's absolutely fantastic! First off, have you seen the pictures? Have you been in the house yet? There's this wall of windows in the living room, overlooking a beautiful backyard. It has granite countertops throughout. There's a massive master closet and tons of storage throughout the home. Everything has been really well taken care of. But don't just take my word for it. In fact, my sellers were so confident of this, they ordered a full inspection report for you before they ever even went live on the market."

At this point, most buyer agents will be shocked. Then the answer continues, "What's your email address? I'll send it over. You're going to love it. There were a few little things on there as is typical for a home this age, but they've already taken care of the major stuff. I'll let you know everything that's already been done. Your buyers can rest easy and know they're getting a great house. Now, we expect this thing to fly off the shelf, so I highly encourage you to come as quickly as you can. Bring us an offer if you're able. I'll let you know if anything changes, but try to get in there quickly because it really may not be available through the weekend."

Notice how the feeling of leverage has instantly shifted from buyer to seller. It all happens as a result of a well-crafted negotiation strategy and implemented marketing plan for the home.

This is just one tiny example of one small piece of an overall negotiation strategy, but you can clearly see how treating every aspect of the advertising, marketing, sales, and communication process as negotiation, or as an opportunity to increase or give away leverage, can add up to massive, record-breaking results.

How do you create a negotiation plan?

When we meet with prospective sellers we often ask, "What plan, process, or system did other agents you've met with or worked with in the past use to market, negotiate, and sell your home?"

Almost exclusively, the answer is some iteration of: "Well, they put a sign in the yard, put it on the MLS, maybe did a Facebook post or two, and an open house if they went above and beyond. Then they waited for phone calls."

The truth is that's pretty much all you're going to get from most real estate agents, no matter how flashy their business card or website is.

Having a well thought-out plan means understanding current buyer trends. This includes economic, political, developmental, financial, and educational movements happening in the hyper-local area near your home and factoring those into the market, the message, and the media used to get attention, interest, and commitments from buyers.

Having a successful plan means considering the thousands of potential actions that could be utilized to sell a home and customizing an approach with the correct few dozen that will drive the desired result in your scenario.

Negotiation Begins on Day 1

A lot of people think negotiation starts once the buyer has submitted their offer, but truthfully it begins long before that. In the modern market, the first view of a home is almost always online.

The way a potential home buyer feels the moment they see a home online is potentially the single most important moment of the negotiation, yet the vast majority of agents are completely absent from that moment in regards to strategy. We've been able to "sell" properties before a buyer even walks in the door. By that time, 80% of the negotiation value or leverage is either used or lost.

The way the buyer feels when they scroll through the photos online, when they step into the house, as well as their interactions on phone calls and emails about the property before they see it, informs their actual experience inside the property, and then their subsequent conversations with their agent, their family, their home inspector, mortgage lender, and whoever else is involved. That's when they are deciding how much they like it, if they want to make an offer, how much to offer on the house, how fast to make an offer, and what else they are willing to do to get to the finish line.

We want to create a scenario where the buyer says, "Oh my goodness. I'm not gonna let go of this doorknob, Mrs. Agent. What do we have to pay to get this house so we don't miss out on it and no one else even gets a chance at it?"

3 Steps to Massive Sales Prices

Most homeowners and agents believe that marketing is completely separate from negotiation and consists only of showing the house in a positive light when taking photos, posting the listing of the property on the internet, and showing it to buyers in person or at an open house.

We believe that's only a fraction of what needs to be done to position the home for maximum success. There are critical strategies both tangible and behind the scenes that have massive impact on a seller's success in achieving their desired result when selling a home. Feel free to view our entire 7-step proprietary marketing and negotiation system which we use to guarantee to sell every home for over the average price and under the average time in video format at www.OverUnderGuarantee.com.

Step 1: Create scarcity

Our goal is not to simply work with the natural scarcity present in any given real estate market. Our goal is to create scarcity where none exists or to create extreme scarcity when it already does exist. We do this by creating what we call "a market of one." A market of one is a market where the buyer has one singular option. If they are not able to purchase the one option, they simply do not get one. There is no alternative.

One of the ways we create scarcity for a buyer is by providing a full pre-inspection report. That way the buyer knows everything about the property before they ever step inside.

The buyer is almost always going to do their own inspection report and find out about the issues with the house, so why let them have all the leverage when it comes time to negotiate repairs?

Having that information up front allows a seller to manage costs, contractors, and avoid paying a premium for the buyers' choice contractors. We can pretty much assure you that yours will be one of the very few homes offering this level of stress-reducing information so early in the process.

A second way we create scarcity is through excellent staging and photography that accentuate the points of scarcity, or niches, in your home. These are the unique features, layout, or combinations of amenities that make your home a market of one. If those are presented at a world-class level by professional stagers trained to know buyer psychology and trends, and photographers skilled at capturing them in a unique way, it will elevate the perception of your home because very few people go through the trouble and spend the money to do both.

Both of these will help the buyer feel like your property is one-of-a-kind, even if it is not. However, there's more than just the buyer involved in the process.

A vast majority of the time a buyer is represented by an agent. That agent has a pretty big role in determining what the buyer will offer, what the buyer thinks, and what kind of repairs the buyer will ask for, because that agent is the professional consultant, walking them through the process.

Remember that front yard conversation? These are the folks who buyers will tell, "Hey, we love this house. What do you think we should offer? Is it priced well?" This gives the agent a lot of say in the process, although the buyer should always make the final call.

Most sellers work, or at least want to work, to creatively incentivize the buyer (through marketing, photos, staging, etc.), but almost never go beyond the norm to incentivize the buyer's agent. That agent typically receives a similar commission, regardless of what property their buyer purchases. Truthfully, they don't have much tendency to lean toward or away from any certain property the buyer wants to see. However, if you incentivize the buyer agent, legally and ethically, all of a sudden, the person who is normally working against you for the length of the transaction... the one who haggles you down asking for more repairs, trying to get the best deal possible for the buyers... will now be motivated to get to closing as much as anyone else in the process.

We do this a few different ways. Specifically, we incentivize agents by offering a travel incentive, say a cruise—a free five-day, four-night cruise for two—not for the buyer, but for the agent who brings the buyer to the property. You may think that sounds expensive for every single transaction, but it can be a very worthwhile investment. Suddenly an agent is literally managing the process on behalf of the buyer. They're now dying to get to closing so they can go on a vacation.

This all creates more desire to show your property, more desire to make a more compelling offer, and a tendency to request fewer repairs so the buyer doesn't get cold feet and walk away. Ultimately it makes a smoother closing process from start to finish, and saves time, money, and stress.

When agents call us, they often ask three exact questions in the same order every time.

- "Hey, I saw your property on Main Street. Is it still available?"

- "Are you working any offers and what kind of activity have you had?"

- Then they'll pause and kind of sheepishly say... "Tell me about that cruise! I've never seen that before. Is that legit? Like, is that a hoax? What's the catch?"

We are now adding value to both the buyer's agent and the buyer. By the time they get to the house they're often already sold and willing to do whatever it takes to lock it down.

My favorite example of how persuasive this technique can be is actually from a client's point of view. I was meeting with a current client not long ago when a call came in from another agent about one of my properties that was for sale. I stepped aside and took the call. I heard exactly where the conversation was going and thought it would be fun to show the clients I was at the house with what the marketing we had discussed days earlier looked like in action.

The agent on the call had started by asking if my property was still available and if I was working any offers. I walked back into the room with my clients and gave them a wink, and put the call on speaker phone. Sure enough, the agent continued with, "Dude, is this for real? You're offering a free cruise on this property? I've never been on a cruise and I've been dying to go. Like literally, what do I have to do?

This house is going to be my clients'. Tell me what we have to do and we'll make it happen."

My new seller just tapped his wife on the arm, like *Holy cow, are you hearing this?* They have now become huge raving fans and send us referrals regularly. It just shows that the system works.

Step 2: Create urgency

This is a simple but overwhelmingly powerful strategy that most sellers and agents alike completely miss. You can create urgency through the language you use in calls, emails, and messages. It creates intense urgency when I tell the buyer or buyer's agent, "Hey look, I can't guarantee anything past 5:00 P.M. this evening. We have a multiple-offer situation. I already have an offer in hand and I'm expecting two more. We've set a date and time and are asking for highest and best bids. Of course, the seller can make a decision to move on any offer at any point. I strongly recommend getting out to the property by the end of the day and placing your offer right away so you guys don't miss out."

But what if you don't have multiple offers? Don't feel like you have to lie to create urgency. Studying the psychology of language, and how to ethically create urgency regardless of how much traffic or activity the property has, is a massive paradigm shift on how this is handled in the industry, and will impact the sale significantly.

Find something true about the situation and let the buyer agent assume the rest. Consider using phrases like, "We have had a ton of buyers reach out," "I expect a ton of showings and offers based on this price in this neighborhood," or "the way things are going in this market,

I would be shocked if it was still available at the end of the weekend."

This kind of conversation sets a fire under the buyer agent. It changes the way they talk with their buyers about the property. "If we don't go now, you're not going to get this house."

Knowing when the bulk of house showings occur in your market and launching your home onto the market at the exact right time to capture rabid interest will drive rapid and attractive offers as well. This is a fantastically simple strategy that a majority of sellers and their agents get wrong.

Creating scarcity and urgency does not have to be difficult or expensive. You as a homeowner can use a similar approach. It doesn't have to be a travel incentive. It could be an experience, cash, or extra commission to the buyer agent. Be creative! But be sure, when used properly and in conjunction with other strategic marketing strategies, it will return its cost multiple times over.

Step 3: Negotiate All the Time

Remember that 80% of the negotiating is already done by the time the buyer steps in the door. The scenario from the beginning of the chapter will move differently if the buyer agent gets the more informative response, along with a pre-inspection report to set the clients' minds at ease, and becomes highly motivated by an incentive directed to the buyer agent.

What is that agent going to say to his clients in the front yard now? "I mean, honestly... Mr. Buyer. I talked with the listing agent yesterday. It sounded like he wanted to buy the house himself. He would not stop going on and on about all the great things. They have a full pre-inspection report for us that we can use. We already know everything there is to know. They said there was a ton of traffic and they're expecting multiple offers. We really need to make this thing happen today because otherwise we may not get it. I'd hate to see you lose out on this beautiful home. I mean, you just walked through it. It's amazing, right?"

You can imagine how the buyer becomes emotionally charged. They're standing in the front yard. They're excited. The agent lays all this on them. And then what happens? They look at each other. The agent adds, "Honestly, I don't even know if a full-price offer is going to get this house. It sounds like it may go above asking. Maybe we should call them back and ask if $315k will get this thing done today."

Literally the only thing that changed in this scenario that happens all the time is the way the listing agent answered the phone call. They weren't talking contracts, pricing terms, or closing dates. It was just a phone call that most agents overlook or get annoyed by, often texting back instead of answering the phone. And this call alone can impact the transaction by 5-10% of the sale price. That's real money.

As you can tell, negotiation is so much more than waiting for an offer and starting to haggle. In our world, we are often thought of as marketers. That is certainly a fair title as we do spend a tremendous amount of time, energy, and resources to identify the ideal buyer market, craft an ideal message for that ideal buyer market, and carefully select the appropriate media (radio, digital, social, print, event, phone, text, voicemail, video, etc.) to deliver that ideal message to the ideal buyer for each home. That is a huge aspect of what we do.

However, the terms *marketing* and *negotiation* begin to blur together when you understand that all marketing is a form of negotiation. Our selection of the right target market, message, and media are all part of communicating value to the most perfect buyer we can identify. That is the buyer who pays the most, the fastest, with the least amount of drama.

So, negotiation becomes the broader term, and marketing, sales, and execution fit inside that more expansive effort.

Executing the plan

It can feel like a complicated process when you're trying to do all these things on your own. It is challenging to do every task at an expert level. There are so many moving pieces. It's tricky to wear all those different hats and try to get everything done at the highest level. And if not, then you're leaving something on the negotiating table.

Between the point you decide to put a home "on the market," and when you close and fund, hundreds of documents with thousands of initials and signatures will be handled by dozens of professionals in dozens of industries and inspected, scanned, emailed, mailed, overnighted, couriered, and hand-delivered all over the world.

Our marketing plan is what causes people to not only see the home online, but favorite it, tour it, and make an offer on it. Likewise, the reason why we get buyers to call about properties, come look at properties, and make high offers is because our team-wide negotiation strategy is calculated at every step of the process. From every angle, we leave no rock unturned. We get as many eyeballs on the property as possible to get the full impact.

These marketing secrets, as we call them, are clearly not that secret. We didn't invent any of the core concepts. However, the way we have customized them for residential real estate, and the way we weave them together in unique ways based on the needs of our sellers and their properties, compounds the benefit exponentially. This is what allows the seemingly routine sale of a home to often transform the lives of our clients.

The value of just having staging and a professional photographer is good. But when you use them together, along with a pre-inspection, marketing the home multiple ways to multiple audiences, negotiate terms masterfully, use communication that creates scarcity and urgency, and execute honestly and ethically with professionalism, it has a huge and tangible impact on the outcome of a transaction. This creates a scenario for any home to sell way above what the neighbors' homes are selling for... and way faster.

This is clearly a multi-faceted system with a tapestry of ideas an individual homeowner could do if you have the time, energy, expertise, and resources to connect to dozens of vendors. It is possible. And we're thrilled to share it with you so you can have the best sale for your home. It may be the only opportunity you'll have in the next 5 to 10 years to maximize the equity in either your largest or most impactful investment in your life—your home.

It's been our experience that having a team working together, committed to this plan (and its constant improvement), who keeps score based on the client's world-class experience is probably the best route for most homeowners. We are each experts in one particular field. Our goal is to get you to the finish line with as much peace of mind and security and financial benefit as possible, and we'd love to help you.

**For world class real estate guidance
in the Dallas & Fort Worth markets,
contact the Todd Tramonte Home Selling Team at
www.ToddTramonteHomeSellingTeam.com
(214) 216-2161**

BONUS CHAPTER

HOW TO MAKE SHORT-TERM VACATION RENTALS WORK

WITH CYNTHIA TANT, PH.D.

DR. CYNTHIA TANT is the Broker/Owner of Gulf Coast Home Experts, sales brokerage, and Gulf Coast Real Estate Management, property management. As owner of Gulf Coast BnB Rentals, short-term vacation rentals, Dr. Tant oversees all three companies for a "One-Stop Shop" client experience. She will sell, buy, invest, rehab, rent, or manage your current or future home(s) and educate you during the process.

With more than 25 years of investment experience and 17 years of retail sales in real estate, Dr. Tant has worked with several thousand clients on their housing needs. Whether it is your first home or your 10th, just getting started with investing or a seasoned pro, she can guide you through the process.

Before real estate, Dr. Tant was in academia, teaching Biomechanics and Statistics, not very relatable experience, but extremely necessary to educating her clients on the real estate process. Her expertise and commitment allowed her to be recognized as Outstanding Professor at two different institutions and 2014 Pensacola WCR Realtor of the Year. Serving as 2016 Pensacola WCR President, she led her network to #1 membership retention in the entire USA WCR for mega chapters.

Living near Pensacola Beach, in her spare time, she loves to be on the water, boating/sailing or traveling to other amazing beaches of the world. Ask Dr. Tant how to create wealth through real estate—it is her secret talent.

www.gulfcoasthomeexperts.com
cindy@move2FLA.com
(850) 393-5134

HOW TO MAKE SHORT-TERM VACATION RENTALS WORK

What kinds of vacation properties are available?

One of the most successful business models now is short-term vacation rentals listed through Airbnb, VRBO, or Booking.com platforms. If you are interested in just one property or developing a portfolio of multiple investment properties, consider the vacation property route.

If you live in a destination town, it is much easier to find those properties, ready to go, that have been used for vacation rentals and can be easily sold as a vacation rental property. Traditional, short-term rental vacation homes are located in beach towns or in the mountains or lake town... basically anywhere people go to vacation.

Imagine all the incredibly unique places for properties that can be visited in a location that may not necessarily be a vacation destination. For example, if people visit Dallas and prefer to not stay in a hotel or condominium, they can rent out a whole house for a wedding. Today's "sharing economy" model has added additional kinds of vacation rentals, like renting out a room in your house or RV... or even something unique like a castle.

How do I get started?

Step 1: Type of property

The first step is to determine what type of property you want, based on the purpose you are going to be using it for. Let's say you would like a week-long rental, with all the amenities—a pool, maybe a tennis court, or more things like that—where families can be involved in everything. When a whole family comes together, they often need a bigger house, like five bedrooms with multiple beds and a fully equipped kitchen.

Finding these properties to invest in is just like locating a house that you would rent long-term, except your plan could be to rent it short-term via the Airbnb or VRBO model.

Higher profitability is going to come from larger luxury homes, with the opportunity to accommodate 15 to 20 people. That also comes with a higher purchase price, but you can leverage a higher return with fewer properties in your portfolio.

If you want to go "big time," statistics show that owning 20 units of 3+ bedrooms would bring in around $1M in revenue. However, if you want to rent to overnight travelers, then smaller studios and 1- to 2-bedroom properties will make more sense. There will be more frequent turnover, but higher occupancy.

There are different niche markets. For example, if you have a property that allows pets, many will pay extra for this privilege. Each niche market has its own unique pluses and minuses.

Keep in mind, you do not have to manage all of this yourself. You can grow your portfolio over time, and also have a local Short-term Rental (STR) property manager helping you create wealth.

Step 2: Type of traveler

Your second step is to identify the type of traveler you want to service, which will inform the type of property you will purchase. They go hand in hand.

The profit potential is highly location-driven. What we have in the Pensacola / Pensacola Beach area will be different from San Diego. There is a much higher average rental price in San Diego, but then you are going to pay a higher purchase price for the property to start with, while the returns may not be as high of a percentage rate.

Earning potential in short-term rentals follows the same principal as in all of real estate—location, location, location—followed by time of year. Is there a seasonality to your preferred location? It is based on size, location, and occupancy. Each property has its areas of town that are in demand, whether it is close to a beach, lake, mountain, downtown area, a military base or something like that, where people are coming into town for different reasons.

Even people who list rooms in their homes that are in the middle of nowhere can get them booked. Vacationers pick a destination, but may not want to pay the higher price to be right on the beach. Or perhaps they want more of a private setting. They might also choose to stay in town and do daytrips to wherever they want to go.

Step 3: Rental income

Your third step will be to determine what is a good rental income for you. For example, if I aimed to bring in 1% of the purchase price per month, and I bought a $300,000 home, I'd like to earn $3,000 a month for it as a 12-month rental.

It is possible to generate 2 to 3 times as much from a short-term rental. If I could bring in 2 to 3 times that for the same property through STR, then I would be in the $6,000 to $9,000 per month range.

Owning 20 properties of three bedrooms or larger will generate, on average, about $50,000 a year each, which gets you to a million dollars. There is some scale to this, but there are also market differences.

Step 4: Selecting a property
After you've made the choice to buy, know the type of guest you want to target, and have determined the type of property and potential income you want, the next step will be to decide where the property will be located.

Many people start investing near their primary residence, for a hands-on approach. Being local gives you an advantage of knowing if your city, town, or region has any restrictions for STR. Or your family might like to visit a vacation destination on an annual basis, and you could purchase your STR property in that town.

How much can you make from short-term rentals?

As you try to figure out your numbers, no doubt you will ask: "How much I can make?" You should also consider any additional expenses you need to be aware of with your selected property.

I advise starting with a Realtor who has experience in short-term rentals and is also as an investor themselves. They will know the ropes in that specific location.

Costs to consider:
Let's begin with expenses associated with buying the property. You will have closing costs, insurance, taxes, and

possibly HOA fees. Another consideration is whether you buying a property that is already furnished and ready to go. In the industry, these are referred to as "turnkey." Some even have future rentals on the books.

Usually an ideal STR property is going to be completely furnished or it's going to be empty. Consider how much it will cost you, all the way down to the knives, forks, and spoons. Is it a studio apartment or a 4-bedroom house? If you are in the luxury market, you better have high-end furnishings. The guest is paying a premium for the property and all the extra perks.

I do provide my buyers with a spreadsheet that helps determine when they will return their investment based on rental projections. If it's a fixer-upper, you will have additional things to consider, making sure it's ready to furnish the house, then market and get it rented.

Another big decision is whether you are going to manage the rental yourself or hire a property manager. There are large vacation rental companies, medium-sized, and smaller companies in every market. If your Realtor also is a property manager and has assisted you through all this, I suggest you give them the business. A manager will run you between 20-35% of the income, depending on location and what services they provide for you.

If you buy it and choose to manage the property on your own, you will need to find cleaners, maintenance people, marketing solutions, answer calls, as well as book guests. This may be manageable on your own if you have just one or two properties, without a full-time job, and you live locally. But if you are out of the area, or have a full-time job, it may be difficult to stay on top of everything.

Sample experience

Let me give you an example of an out-of-state investor of a Pensacola Beach vacation rental. This investor wished to have the property for the family to visit several times each year, but then fully managed by a property manager the rest of the time.

In summary, the five things we do at Gulf Coast Home Experts and Gulf Coast BNB Rentals for super successful and happy vacation homeowners, are as follows:

1. **Hire a real estate professional with investment and short-term rental experience**. Even better, hire one who has companies established to fulfill all your needs. Vacation rentals are a different animal because you do have things that come up like insurance, repairs, accidents, and HOA fees. Finding that real estate professional, who you can work with, who knows the market and then identify the type of home, or condo you want to purchase.

2. **What is the price range now in your area of choice?** Location is key. A Gulf-front 3-bedroom condo directly on the water, in a high floor location, will cost you upwards of $600,000 to purchase. However, average rental rates are $400-$500 a night, with a typical week during the high season bringing in $4,000 for special event weeks. As a vacation destination beach town, Pensacola Beach has many condominiums. Unfortunately, mortgage lenders are not really lender friendly right now for condominiums, so many investors do pay cash or use self-directed IRAs. Your Realtor should have basic knowledge in this area.

They may identify it as a second-home investment. Then we've got more flexibility on where to go and what to do. With your real estate professional, go through the properties that are available. If it is a turnkey in move-in shape, then you can work the numbers and make your decision.

3. **You own a vacation rental, but who is going to manage it?** Hopefully, you thought of this up front and hired the Realtor I suggested with the experience you need. If the property has been rented in the past, you'll have a track record of how much income was procured. If not, you and your Realtor will start from scratch and give an estimate, or potential of what returns you might expect. And then you can start renting it out.

   The rental manager will be paid between 20-35% of the income, off the top. A good manager will make your life happy. They will take care of all the issues that might arise and send you a check at the end of the month.

4. **Short-term property managers are not housekeepers, maintenance repair folks, pest control, or police.** However, they do employ the people to take care of your property. A good property manager will have excellent reviews from past guests. They will have a developed network of folks who have been screened to service your property for excellence. Yes, damage can occur, and police may need to be contacted. The first person called will be your property manager, not you. If you don't believe you are receiving the service you are paying for, shop around. Find the company for you.

5. **Time to buy another.** You selected the right property, in the right area, with the right real estate professional. Your property manager has been amazing, and your returns were better than expected. Pull the trigger and let's start again. Maybe, you might think of a retirement home, that you purchase while you are employed and rent it out short-term for now, so you can come and visit. Imagine being able to stay in your own investment property whenever you want instead of having to ensure you have a long-term tenant at all times in order to meet your financial obligations on the property.

The future of STRs

What will the future hold for short-term vacation rentals? Take a glance at history. Crises and disasters have continually set the stage for change, often for the better. There is every reason to believe the short-term rental market will be around in the future. There will always be a need for short-term stays in homes, apartments, condos, B&Bs, beach houses, and villas. Thousands of hotels all over the world are expected to shut down due to the COVID-19 crisis which means less accommodation supply, which in turn means increased demand for STRs.

The mindset of the community or government sometimes feels that properties in the STR market are taking away housing that people could live in on a full-time basis. Some bigger cities are not short-term rental friendly for this reason. Check with your local rules and regulations, pay your vacation rental taxes, and run this as a business. Better yet, find a STR property manager in the area you are looking to invest and let them manage it for you.

Airbnb, VRBO, and Booking.com have disrupted the accommodations market, and not everyone is happy about that. But you as the investor can take advantage of the Airbnb mission: "Belong Anywhere." Airbnb's biggest disruption is that it has enabled anyone to become a micro-hotelier, the same way that Uber enabled anyone to become a driver. Not only does this create income opportunities for people, but it creates a dynamic supply of accommodations. Airbnb has already opened a whole new part of the lodging industry, and it's only going to get bigger as the entire sharing/collaborative economy continues to grow. So why shouldn't you have a piece of it!

Selecting a Realtor

There are not too many real estate professionals with STR investing and property management experience, so it may take time to locate the right one. Or contact me, and I will be glad to share my rolodex with you of real estate pros from around the world.

Pensacola is a destination, small-town vacation spot, so we like short-term rentals. It brings more people into the community, hence increased revenue for our city. Many bigger cities, in condominiums, apartment complexes or residential communities with HOAs, however, have put restrictions on individual owners of STR.

As a resident of Pensacola, FL, I manage both long-term and short-term rental properties. Here in my market, we are at the crossroads of affordability and marketability. We have the beaches, the Blue Angels, the military, a historic downtown and tons of beach and downtown festivals. We also have two smaller colleges and a state university, plus a double-A baseball team—Blue Wahoos—and winning Ice Flyers hockey team, and professional beach volleyball tournaments. Our area is home to all kinds of water events, boating, scuba and fishing. Also, a lively jazz community, downtown arts, museums, and opera draw many visitors each year.

Our signature events are Pensacon, two Blue Angels shows, Mardi Gras, City of Five Flags Celebration, Crawfish Festival, Bands on the Beach, Pensacola Seafood Festival, Crawfish Festival, Pensacola Interstate Fair, Frank Brown Songwriters Fest, Interstate Mullet Toss, Foo Foo Fest, Gallery Night, Greater Gulfcoast Arts Festival and Winterfest. There are a host of amazing restaurants and local brew pubs downtown and on the beach. Look at what the community offers, and ask yourself why people would come to visit that location.

With almost year-round desirable, warm weather in Pensacola, you can buy below $300,000 make a return of $30k-50k per year. Start looking around for the places you like to vacation. If you are looking for a mountain town—like Vail, CO—it may be too restrictive because of purchase price. But if you could be in a lesser-known town that still has marketable draws, that's where those crossroads between affordability and marketability will intersect.

Allow me to find your perfect Short-Term Vacation Rental investment. LEARN MORE about our area and the services I provide at www.YourGulfCoastLifestyle.com. Visit and register, you will receive a Digital Guidebook of one of my vacation rentals on Pensacola Beach. I would love to show you "My Beach."

Made in the USA
Monee, IL
12 July 2021